AMBER

SKY

BY

A.R. DASH

AMBER SKY
A.R. DASH

AMBER SKY
A.R. DASH

COPYRIGHT ©2014 BY ARMEIN PURCELL

For permission to do otherwise please contact the
author at (armein_purcell@yahoo.com)

If you are unable to order this book from your local
bookstore, this book can be ordered online from
Amazonbooks.com

ISBN:9780991584949

Cover Design by: Cue Mc Boo

Editor: Armein Purcell

AMBER SKY
A.R. DASH

ACKNOWLEDGEMENTS

To my wonderful children Arjon and Zshquan.

Sometimes the longest journey in life is the distance between people...But rest assured that I am on my way... And this time, I've finally gotten it right.

To Crystal Upchurch:

In the depths of my despair and as the weight of the world grew heavier, not only did you take the time to help me keep my spirits up, but you also urged me to keep my eyes on the prize... I will never forget that... I am not sure of what legacy you plan to leave, but I thought it only right to let the world know that you are amazing... Thank you... And by the way, I can't wait to see what you guys do with that book. Good Luck and best wishes with that. I'll be rooting for you guys from the stands.

To Christine Moody:

Thank you for always reminding me that what's for me, is for me, and there is nothing that anyone can do about it.

To Mama Shirley and the Maxwell Family:

Thank you for extending so much love to my sister. I am forever grateful.

To Kissy Maxwell:

Always remember; if it doesn't feel right, it's probably not. But if it feels like the answer, don't question it.

To all who love me:

Just remember that our time is coming; thank you all for not giving up on me the way so many others have.

And to my Lord and Savior:

You have cleansed my soul and filled me with love. I've made many mistakes and will probably make many more. But through it

AMBER SKY
A.R. DASH

all, it is the strength that you give to me that allows me to walk with
my head held high... You have made me anew... Thank You for
your mercy.

AMBER SKY
A.R. DASH

Like every other girl in the world, Amber Sky just wants to be happy. She is young, full of ambition and very beautiful; but her beauty cannot save her from the ugliness of the world.

She fights desperately to get ahead in life, and the only weapon she has, is her *GIRL POWER!!!*

CHAPTER

1.

AMBER SKY
A.R. DASH

The lump in her throat grew. Tightly she held the stack of books against her chest. Twenty-two year old Amber Sky felt like the walls were closing in on her.

"Please mommy! Please! Don't do this to me again!"

Her mother Charlene, moved about the room gathering her belongings as if the situation was of no urgency. She didn't even bother to look at Sky. The stinging feeling behind Sky's eyes caused her to blink and to take a deep breath. There was no way that she would give her mother the satisfaction of seeing tears fall down her face.

Sky's skin felt like it was on fire as she watched her mother in disbelief. Her dreams to be a nurse were dying right there in front of her and all she could do was swim in the feeling of hopelessness that filled her body.

In one last cry of despair, she let out a plea that came from the bottom of her heart.

"Please Mommy, don't make me miss another day of school. If I do, I will be kicked out of the nursing program"

Her mother took a large purse into her hand and finally turned and met eyes with Sky. For a second Sky thought she saw a bit of compassion in her mother's face. She was wrong.

"Sky please, stop being so dramatic. Those people are not going to kick you out of that program for missing a few days of class. And if they do, than you don't need that kind of a program anyway. It's no good for you, trust me, I know. They should know that people have lives outside of their program, and besides, I really need you to stay home to babysit your sisters. I promise you that this will be the last time."

"But---"

Was the only word Sky could get out. She let her books fall to her side then her shoulders fell as if there was no more air in her body. Sky stood in the middle of the living room wearing a pair of blue nursing scrubs that she would probably be wearing for the last time. Her jaws were tight.

Sky's nine month old sister Lilly sat up in her baby chair on top of the coffee table sucking on a pacifier and looking around the room with curious eyes. Autumn, the thirteen year old middle child sat on the couch closest to the baby with a worrisome look on her face. In what looked like an attempt to avoid eye contact with Sky, she nervously played with the baby Lilly's feet. It appeared as though she felt like she was the cause for the dispute by having to be babysat by her older sister.

And Dustin, the mother's current fiancé, and father of baby Lilly, stood at the front door holding it open with one hand and holding a burning cigarette with the other. The twist of his lip and the way he continuously huffed made it clear that he was ready to go.

He mumbled underneath his breath.

"Oh boy, I wish you come on already."

Quickly Charlene opened her oversized imitation Coach bag and began to fumble through it without raising her head. Dustin's eyes stalked her and it was plain to see that she knew it. Sky couldn't help but to shake her head in disgust.

Dustin cleared his throat. His words were demanding.

"Charlene! We have to get going! How many times do I have to tell you that I can't be late!"

Charlene looked more like a servant then she did a fiancé.

She spoke as if she were afraid to say the wrong thing.

"Okay, Okay, Okay... I'm coming right now. Just go and start the car, I will be out there in a minute."

9

She reached into her bag and pulled out a set of keys then tossed them to him. He caught them and then walked out of the house with a slam of the door behind him. The bang of the door caused Charlene's shoulder's to jump and it startled baby Lilly. Lilly let out a loud cry.

Charlene pulled a matching purse out of her Coach bag and at the same looked at her daughter Autumn with an unexpected attitude.

"Why are you just sitting there looking silly? Pick her up and give her a bottle."

Autumn rolled her eyes but did as she was told.

Charlene opened the small purse and pulled out a twenty dollar bill. She looked at Sky but paused before approaching her oldest child. Sky was completely crushed on the inside but she stood there with her head held high. There was only about a six step space between her and her mother, but Sky had never felt more distant from the lady in all of her life.

Charlene stepped directly in front of her and held out the money.

"Get Lilly some diapers and some baby wipes, then with the change, get Autumn something to eat; a turkey and cheese sandwich from the corner store or something like that. That should hold her until I get back. I'm only going to be a couple of hours."

Sky wanted to say something, but because of the bitter taste in her mouth, she held her tongue. Charlene must've felt the tension. She raised her eyebrows as if she dared Sky to anything out of the way. Sky reached out and pulled the money from her mother's hand with a little force.

Charlene reacted with a quick temper.

"Don't be snatching nothing from me!"

"I didn't snatch it!"

Charlene moved so close to Sky that it caused Sky to take a step back. She pointed an angry finger into her daughters face.

"I don't know who you think you raising your voice at! You must've lost your damned mind!"

Sky stood there with a stone face. From outside of the house the sound of a horn began to blare like crazy. Charlene's neck snapped towards the window and robotically she stepped towards the door. Just before she walked out of the house she looked back at Sky.

"And clean this house up too. I want it spotless by the time I get back."

Then she left the house without another word.

Sky didn't need a mirror to know that her face was beet red. She could feel the blood in her cheeks. Unconsciously her feet moved across the room towards the living room window. Her motions were zombie like. She was so lost in her thoughts that she forgot her siblings were in the room with her.

Sky pulled the living curtain back just in time to see her mother step up into the passenger side of her own S.U.V. Sky's nose flared up. She couldn't believe that her mother was still allowing Dustin to drive. He'd recently accumulated over five hundred dollars in traffic tickets; a bill that fell on Charlene. And worse than that, he didn't even possess a valid driver's license. The S.U.V. jerked, and then sped away from the curb. Sky's blood pressure rose from hot to a boil.

She really didn't understand what her mother saw in Dustin. The so-called man couldn't even hold a job. To Sky he was nothing more than a loser and a user. The reason why he was rushing Charlene out of the house was because he had to be up at the city welfare building at a certain time so that he could re-apply for governmental assistance. To call him a loser was an understatement.

Charlene was putting Dustin before Sky and to Sky it hurt. But the real reason she was upset was because her and her mother was supposed to be honoring an agreement they made between each other. The agreement was that as long as Sky was in school full time and occasionally helped her mother out around the house then she could live under her mother's roof until she was finished with school and found a job.

Sky realized all too late that her mother's intentions were not at all to help Sky, but instead, they were meant to trap her. And her mother's plan was working perfectly. The reality of the thought tore at Sky's chest and pierced her heart. And Dustin was to blame.

Sky already had personal reasons for disliking the man, but situations like this one put her on the verge of hating him. And to hate someone was something that her father spent years teaching her not to do.

Sky's father was a Caucasian man and her mother was an African-American woman. The world did indeed for whatever reason have a problem with them being together but Sky's father was a strong man that stood up for what he loved and believed in. anytime someone did or said something against Sky or her family, her father would handle the situation immediately. And no matter how much disrespect people shot in their direction, when it was said and done, her father always came back and told her that everyone deserves forgiveness because everyone makes mistakes.

Sky fought tooth and nail with herself to try to live by her father's teachings. But Dustin was pushing it.

Sky stared out of the window aimlessly. Her mind wrestled to come up with something that she could tell the program director so that she wouldn't be terminated from the nursing program, but her mind drew a blank. Lying was also something that her father taught against and as a result, Sky was a horrible liar. She was terrible at trying to look someone in the face while speaking words that weren't true.

Reality hit her like a ton of bricks. Her dreams of having a good job and moving her siblings to a better environment had just been crushed by Charlene the evil witch and her dizzy sidekick Dusty Dustin.

The thought of the silly superhero names caused a light laughter to escape from the clump of sadness in Sky's chest.

Autumn must've taken the sound of her sister's laughter as a sign that it was okay to speak.

Her words were cautious.

"Are you okay Sky?"

Sky wiped away the gloom from her face and turned around to her sisters as if nothing had just happened.

"Of course I am okay."

Sky made it her business to never let her younger siblings see her worried or depressed. And over the years she'd become very good at covering up her pain. She'd hid the pain that she felt when her father died; she hid the pain she felt from witnessing how her mother allowed herself to be treated by the men she involved herself with after her father died; she'd bottled up pain from her own dealings with no good guys; and she even hid the pain she felt from knowing that her siblings were being raised in an unhealthy environment that she couldn't get them away from.

Her siblings were part of the reason why she so desperately wanted to become a nurse. The plan was to become a nurse, save up some money and then to take her siblings away from their mother. But now, she was stuck between a rock and a hard spot and forced to figure out what her next move was. So yeah, Sky had learned how to hide the pain well, but the pain never seemed to end.

Sky placed her books on the edge of the couch and walked over to where her sisters were sitting. Autunm sat there timidly and held Lilly in her arms and fed her a bottle. Sky reached out for the baby and looked into Autumns face.

"Stop looking so sad lil' sis. I told you, I'm alright. Like I always tell you, don't waste your energy worrying about me. I'm going to always be okay no matter what. You just make sure you keep on doing what you have to do in school so you don't have to deal with this kind of madness when you get older."

Autumn turned her lips up into a slight smile and nodded her head.

"I will."

"You promise?"

"Um-hmm."

"Good."

Then Autumn looked away from Sky and got up and left the room without saying anything else.

"Umm... Okay." Said Sky.

She didn't understand why Autumn had left the room but she gave it no further thought. She turned her attention to Lilly and the almost empty bottle let Sky know that she was ready to be burped. She took the bottle away from Lilly's suction like lips and sat it on the coffee table. Playfully she raised the infant into the air. Lilly smiled and exposed a mouth full of gums. The sight bought joy to Sky's heart.

"Look at you- look at you- look at the pretty baby."

Lilly smiled harder. Sky toyed with her in the air for a minute and then she sat down and placed Lilly on her lap. Lightly she patted the baby's back. Sky felt a rumble on her leg then Lilly burped.

Sky couldn't help but to laugh.

"It's coming out of both ends huh baby?"

Lilly smiled and Sky laughed harder. She laid Lilly across the couch so that she could change the dirty diaper. As soon as she opened it, the room was overtaken by the smell of baby poop.

"Whoo." Joked Sky.

Lilly giggled as if here scent was funny and her cute dimples and gummy smile continued to soothe Sky's soul.

Sky couldn't understand how someone as beautiful as Lilly was able to come from such an ugly person as Dustin was. And Sky wasn't talking about his looks either, because he wasn't a bad looking man. Although he often looked as though he could use a shower and a shave, when he did get himself together, he was a strong seven on a scale of one to ten.

What made him horrible was his ways and actions. He lived as if he'd had absolutely no home training. Sky thought her mother had completely lost her mind when she started dealing with him. As far as Sky was concerned, Lilly was the only good thing to come out of the dysfunctional relationship. Every time that Sky tried to analyze the situation, she'd find herself further and further behind the eight ball.

First off, her mother was forty-one and Dustin was twenty-eight. And that's not to say that anything is wrong with their age difference, but the problem was that Dustin was an immature twenty-eight year old.

Her mother liked to take her time to get dressed and Dustin would throw on anything or sometimes he would just wear his clothes for days on end. Her mother got up off her behind every day and went to work to make sure the bills were paid, while Dustin sat around all day doing nothing but waiting for the beginning of each month so that he could collect his welfare check. All day long he ran in and out of the house with a bunch of his friends. Sky couldn't stand it so she locked herself in her room when her mother wasn't around. But what Sky disliked the most about her supposed to be step father was the fact that not only did his friends hit on her, but secretly, when no one was around, Dustin did as well.

The thought made Sky's stomach to feel queasy.

Often times Sky brought the issues up to her mother but her mother always found a way to flip the situation to make it seem like Sky was to blame because of the way she dressed.

*

The confrontations between her and her mother would usually start off with Sky approaching Charlene is a respectful manner in an attempt to inform her of some inappropriate thing that Dustin or one of his friends had said or done to her. Charlene never saw it Sky's way.

"If you stop wearing those short shorts and little shirts, maybe you wouldn't receive so much unwanted attention."

Her mother's words felt like the lashing of a whip but Sky always tried to get her mother to understand her point of view.

"But Mom?" she would cry. *"I'm inside of the house that I live in when I am dressed like that. You make it sound like I parade around the streets half naked looking for attention. You know in your heart that that's not the case. When Dustin and his friends are here, I barely come out of my room! Why can't you accept the fact that Dustin and his friends are nothing but pervert? You know it! You just act like you don't because you are always at work."*

AMBER SKY
A.R. DASH

"You are not always in your room. Dustin is constantly telling me how he feels like you are trying to entice him and his friends while I am at work."

"He's lying! Does he tell you how he's always got a house full of people? How all of them are always staring at me and saying degrading things? Including him? Huh Mom? Does he tell you that?"

By this stage of the argument it always seemed like Sky had the upper hand because Charlene was all but speechless. And that's when Sky would really try to get her mother to see what was going on in her absence.

"It's really creepy Mom! They should all not only have more respect for me, but more respect for you! I'm your daughter! And let's not forget about the fact that Autumn can fit all of my clothing. She's only thirteen and she fills the clothes out as well as I do if not better! What? You don't think that they are sneaking looks at her? Well guess what? They are! And I know this because I catch them when they are doing it! But you wouldn't know any of this because you're always at work. I bet Dustin doesn't tell you any of this, does he?"

This is where the conflict would usually come to an end. Charlene's bothered facial expression usually betrayed anything else she tried to say. Her words made it sound as if she didn't believe any of what Sky was telling her, but her face told a different story. In Charlene's face, Sky could tell that her mother believed it all and may even have felt sorry that she wasn't doing anything about it. Sky would leave her mother in the middle of the living room with her thoughts and go into her bedroom and lock the door behind her. Now it was Sky who stood in the middle of the living room lost in thoughts.

*

Lilly had fallen asleep in Sky's arms and Sky decided to take her into the bedroom so that she could start cleaning her mother's house. She stepped into her room and found Autumn curled up on her bed. Sky smiled and laid Lilly next to her sister. Then she left the room to go and do the cleaning.

Sometimes Sky felt like Cinderella. Hopefully her Prince Charming was on his way to rescue her...

CHAPTER 2.

A couple of days dragged by since Sky had been kicked out of Nursing School. The Programs Director called to inform her that she'd been dropped from the program and Sky didn't know what to do so she barricaded herself up in her room. There was no longer a reason for her to go outside. To be a nurse was what she wanted to do with her life ever since she was a little girl. The thought of being able to get up every day knowing that she was going to, in some way, help somebody out in the world, filled her heart with excitement. Getting paid for it was an added bonus. But now she couldn't help anyone, and in fact, she was the one who needed help.

Sky laid across her bed covered by a dark shadow. Gently, with her thumb and her index finger, she rubbed the Diamond encrusted butterfly pendant that hung from the thin gold chain around her neck. The piece of jewelry was the most valuable possession in her life. It may have only been worth a couple of hundred dollars to the world, but to her, it was priceless. The butterfly pendant held so much value because it was the last thing her father had given to her before he so unexpectedly lost his life.

She stared up at the ceiling. A tiny paint chip hanging directly over her threatened to fall and she made a promise to herself not to move if it did. Maybe the dime sized chip would knock some kind of idea into her head of what she should do with her life. She had to do something. The future of her and her sibling's wellbeing depended on it. The weight of the world that she carried on her shoulders suddenly grew heavier.

Sky needed someone to talk too. She thought about her boyfriend Josh, but to call him would be useless. He was at work and was not allowed to carry a phone around with him. He'd told her that he worked for a major construction company and one of the policies was that the employees weren't allowed to carry phones on their person around the sites. He said something about how cell phones had caused previous accidents therefore, they'd been banned.

The thought of Josh made her think about their relationship, or *situationship,* as she liked to call it. Their relationship was more of a physical nature than it was an emotional one. He was eight years older than her and they had been dating for the past six months. Things were kind of cool but as of lately, Sky found herself wanting more than what he was offering. She could easily admit that she had strong feelings for him but she wasn't in love. The situation was becoming a burden to her because just like every other girl in the world, Sky wanted someone of her own so that she could love them and they could love her back. This wasn't really the case with Josh.

She was far from a fool and clearly she could see that her and Josh were not headed in that direction. She even considered breaking things off with him. But somewhere inside of her there was a spark of hope that told her that Josh could be her knight and shining armor, and when the time was right, he was going to help her and her sibling's get away from what Sky called the House of Horrors. And another reason she didn't want to leave him alone was because he was amazing in bed.

Unconsciously a small smile crept across her face and words just blurted out of her mouth.

"Maybe I will break it off next month if things don't get better. But as of now, I need that man."

She felt a tingle inside of her and jumped up off of the bed and moved towards her night stand. *'hopefully he'll see my message and give me a call as soon as he turns his phone on'* she thought to herself. She grabbed her Galaxy cell phone and wondered if her mother was going to pay the bill for the following month.

"Whatever." She said out loud. "If she do, then she do and if she don't she don't. I'll have me a job by then anyway."

Sky looked down at her phone and what she saw made her heart thump underneath her vocal cords. Her ex-friend Danielle had sent her a friend request through Facebook. Sky's mouth dropped open and her eye brows arched as high as they could. Danielle was the only person that Sky ever had a physical fight with. She read the message from her one time friend and really didn't know what to think. *'Hey girl! What's up? Long time no see! gimme a call.'* Sky read the phone number and saw that it was the same cellphone number Danielle had when they were kids. Sky hadn't thought about Danielle since she moved from Staten Island six years ago.

Sky let the hand that was holding the phone fall into her lap and she held lifted her head up. The paint chip was still hanging. When she brought her eyes down she looked directly across her room into the full length mirror hanging from her closet door. *'It's been almost six years, why are you reaching out to me after so much time and acting like we didn't have a huge fallout in front of everybody we know.'*

Sky put the phone down on the bed. Slowly she approached the mirror and looked herself up and down. She wondered if Danielle was still as beautiful as she used to be. Danielle was not only pretty but she was also one of those young girls who developed way before she should have.

Sky use to envy her back then, but now things were different. Sky had grown a lot since the last time she saw her old friend. She was no longer the skinny girl that Danielle knew. Instead, she was a grown woman with a body to match.

Sky examined herself and saw that she was beautiful. She was twenty-two but still had the face of a sixteen year old princess. Her lovely oval face had deep and sexy dimples and her eyes looked like drops of sweet dark honey. She smiled and revealed a perfect set of pearly whites. Her five foot four hundred and thirty five pound frame was to die for. The halter top and boy shorts she had on revealed skin so light that it looked like she could have been a white girl but was kissed by just the right amount of sun for her to be able to pass for a red bone. Her shoulder length hair was a natural mixture of black at the roots and streaks of rusty red down to her ends.

Sky turned to the side and sized up her body. Her stomach was wash board flat and her b-cup breast was a little more than enough to fill a hand. Sky squeezed her breast together and laughed. The she poked her butt out. She didn't have a flat butt, but her butt didn't stick out all crazy either. Overall, she looked good.

The lighting in the room caused a glare from the butterfly pendant sitting between her cleavage to catch her attention. She reached up and touched it lightly. Suddenly her mind was filled with memories of her sweet sixteen birthday party. Not only was that the day her father gave her the necklace, but it was also the day that her and Danielle's friendship came to a sudden end.

*

Sky's birthday is May 29th. And the year of her sixteenth birthday, it fell on Memorial Day. Her mother and father decided to give her an outdoor sweet sixteen party combined with a Memorial Day celebration.

The section of the park where the event was being held was roped off and packed with people. Everybody from both sides of the family seemed to be in attendance. There was also a bunch of people that no one knew scattered throughout the engagement. The sky was clear and bright, the weather was soft and warm and a calm breeze flowed throughout the park.

About a half of acre of manicured grass was beautifully decorated with pink and white tables and chairs creating a pathway. In the middle of the two rows, there laid a royal pink carpet that led up to a small stage. Sitting at the front of the stage was a podium with the name AMBER SKY hand carved across the front of it. Her dad had done the hand carving himself. The entire set up was perfectly arranged for Sky to make her grand entrance.

AMBER SKY
A.R. DASH

It was exactly twelve forty-five and Sky was due to arrive at one o'clock sharp. Whispers spread through the crowd that she would no doubt be late. Everybody that knew Sky knew that she had a serious problem when it came to managing time. Some of her family and friends even joked that she would be late for her own funeral. The closer the clock ticked to one o'clock, the more unsettling the crown grew.

Kathreen, one of Sky's aunts, sprang up from her seat with a wobble. She reached out and grabbed the chair in front of her to steady herself. The party hadn't even officially started and she was already on the verge of being wasted. She looked around to see if anyone had noticed her, then she straightened out her dress and stepped onto the pink carpet.

Kathreen had on a two piece white and pink skirt set that looked ten years to small. The outfit clung to her so tightly that it revealed love handles up top, and dimples down bottom. Everybody stopped what they were doing and looked in her direction. Her first two or three steps were off balance but she gained control of herself quickly. There were a few snickers, but they only served to encourage her onward. She straightened her shoulders and held her chin up high, and then she marched down the pink carpet like she was on a catwalk. From somewhere in the crowd there was a voice.

"Work it girl!"

Kathreen threw her hips from side to side and owned the moment of attention. Nobody could tell aunty Kat that she wasn't fine. She was a fierce forty year old cougar who lived like she was in the prime of her life. And she had no problem getting up in any females face and saying something like:

"Heffa if you play with me, I'm going to take your man home with me, and by this time tomorrow, he will know a new trick."

Then she would claw at the air like a cat and let out a long growl.

"grrrrrr."

The way the 'R rolled off of her tongue had a strange hint of sex appeal to it.

Sky's mother and father stopped the conversation they were having with Sky's teenage boyfriend Eric and Sky's father bounced up from his seat.

"Charlene, what is your crazy sister up to now?"

Charlene shook her head slowly. Then she grabbed her husband by the arm and pulled him close.

"David, please don't let her get you worked up. She doesn't mean any harm."

David smiled his million dollar smile and patted the top of his wife's hand.

"I know she don't honey. But let me stop her before she makes a complete fool of herself. I promise not to embarrass her."

Charlene let go of his arm.

"Thank you David."

Swiftly, David walked towards the stage and Charlene stood up to see what was about to happen. Eric took the distraction as an opportunity to slip away from Sky's parents. He eased away from Charlene's turned back and walked directly over to where a group of the neighborhood girls were sitting.

By the time Charlene noticed he was gone, he was already sitting all up in a Sky's friend Danielle face. Charlene had heard things about Danielle and she really didn't like the fact that Sky was starting to hang out with the girl. Charlene made a mental note to remember to have a talk with Sky. Suddenly,

25

the sound of Kathreen's voice blaring through the microphone caused Charlene to snap her neck towards the stage.

"S'cuse me... S'cuse me everyone. Can I have your attention?"

Kathreen took the microphone into her hand but didn't have time to say another word. In the blink of an eye, David was up on the stage beside her gently prying the microphone out of her hand. Once he had the mic, he covered the top of it and leaned towards Kathreen and whispered something into her ear. She screwed her face up at him, then waved her hand and walked away. David waited until she was completely off of the stage before he looked into the crowd. He stood on the stage alone looking exceptional. He was what you called a white man with swag. He looked like he was dressed to do a cover shoot for a G.Q. Magazine.

His crisp white button down shirt was tucked into a pair of exact fitting thirty six inch waist matching white slacks; neatly, the perfectly cuffed white slacks overlapped a shiny pair of pink and white Patten leather loafers; and his nylon pink and white tie complimented his pink and white checker board belt fabulously. Sky's favorite colors were pink and white so it was only right that David colored the world that color on her special day.

David commanded the crowd's attention and spoke some beautiful words about his daughter who was due to arrive any minute. Charlene noticed that his speech had everyone's attention except for Eric .Eric was too busy sniffing Danielle's tail to notice anything else that was going on around him.

Rumor was that Danielle went around the neighborhood taking all of the boy's virginity and it really was none of Charlene's business but she wanted to know why Eric was so focused on her if he was supposed to be Sky's boyfriend. Charlene eased close enough to Eric and Danielle to hear what they were talking about. And boy did she get an ear full.

AMBER SKY
A.R. DASH

"Come on Danielle." Whined Eric. *"Why are you acting like this? Why won't you answer my calls or talk to me when I see you? What did I do to make you so mad at me?"*

At first Danielle didn't say a word. She just sat there with her arms folded beneath her chest looking like an angry statue. And then, from the corner of her eye, she spotted Charlene eavesdropping on them. She pretended not to see Charlene and looked up at Eric and rolled her eyes.

"What do you mean why am I not talking to you? What about Sky? Isn't she your girlfriend? I just saw you over there having a nice little heart to heart with her parents. You act like you want some of this, but what's up with that?"

Danielle rolled her eyes again but this time she did it with just enough cut of her eye to see if Charlene was still paying attention and she was. Sadly, Eric fell for the trap.

"You already know I really don't like Sky like that. The only reason I hang around her is because I want her to do my homework and stuff like that, and I'm only over there talking to her parents because they paid me to be her date for this stupid party."

Charlene couldn't believe her ears and she wanted to say something but the clock struck one and the sound of loud music let her know that Sky had arrived. Charlene was highly bothered by what she'd heard but there was much of anything that she could do about it at the moment. Sky was expecting Eric to be right there when she arrived so Charlene swallowed her pride and ran over to Eric and pulled him by the arm.

"Come on Eric, Sky's expecting you to be one of the first people that she sees."

She shot Danielle an unpleasant glare then she led Eric down to the beginning of the carpet.

Danielle sat there with a wicked smirk. Her reason for being so cruel was because like many other kids, she was jealous and envied Sky. Sky was disliked by any kid who had it rough because Charlene and David were role model parents that gave their daughter the world. And not only that, but although they lived in a neighborhood full of diverse cultures, Sky had the only bi-racial family in the neighborhood. Not to mention that she was extra pretty. Sky took a lot of heat for that. She was always the best dressed and the prettiest no matter what the occasion was and Danielle hated it. This was her chance at payback and she was going to enjoy every moment of it.

Everyone was staring towards the entrance of the park. A beautiful white carriage was being pulled by two bleach white horses and a man sitting at the front of the carriage dressed in an all-white tuxedo with an all-white top hat. Everyone rose to their feet. The carriage looked like it had been snatched straight out of a fairytale. It was snow white with pink lining its every edge. The large wooden wheels were also white and rolled graciously towards the path of the pink carpet. The scene was perfect.

The entire crowd appeared to be excited to witness Sky in all of her glory. The only stale face belonged to Danielle. She didn't even bother to stand up out of her seat. Her face was tight with anger as her eyes beamed at the horse and carriage arrangement.

Cameras started flashing and people recorded images of the scene from their cell phones like they were paparazzi's and Sky was a superstar.

David, Charlene and Eric stood there waiting for Sky to exit the chariot. The chauffeur climbed down from his seat and opened the carriage door for Sky. A white gloved hand reached out of the door and the chauffeur politely took it into his own. Carefully he escorted Sky down from the carriage.

Sky was breath taking. Her strapless gown was as pure white as the carriage, and just like the carriage, it was lined with pink. Her white gloves extended to her elbows and her custom made white shoes were prettier that Dorothy's glass slippers.

She stood in front of her chariot stiff from all of the chants of the crowd. Then she shook off the nervous feeling and smiled a brilliant smile. Her head looked from one side of the park to the other and she was pleased with the turn out of the event.

The Chauffeur handed Sky over to her father and then took a bow and backed away gracefully.

David smiled from ear to ear.

"Look at my little princess. You are beautiful."

The sight of her father gave Sky extra confidence.

"Thank you Daddy."

He leaned in and kissed her on the cheek then he let her hand go and took a step back. Then he bent down in front of her and reached into his breast pocket. He smiled proudly and pulled out a rectangular jewelry box. The crowd grew quiet.

David opened the box and Sky saw the expensive looking thin gold chain with the diamond encrusted pendant attached to it. Sky gasped and her hands flew up and covered her mouth.

David took the necklace from the box and stood up.

"Turn around my lovely."

Sky was about to do as she was asked but from out of nowhere, Danielle came storming down the pink carpet with evil in her eyes. The crowd stopped taking pictures and it was clear that everyone knew something bad was about to happen.

Danielle stopped directly in front of Eric. The blood disappeared from Eric's face.

Sky was confused. "What's going on Danielle?"

Danielle cut her eyes at Sky and ignored her as if she hadn't said anything. She turned to Eric.

Her words were icy cold. "I'm ready to go Eric."

It was so quiet that a pin could be heard if it hit the grass.

Then Eric did the unthinkable. Without second thought, he looked Sky square in the eyes.

"Sky, I'm sorry but I have to be going?"

Sky's heart hammered in her throat. Eric stepped away from Charlene's side over to where Danielle was standing and the two of them turned and began to walk away.

Sky's entire body burned with anger. For the first time in her life, she shouted out a disrespectful word in front of her parents.

"You little slut!"

Sky moved with cat quick feet and launched at Danielle. Danielle's back was turned and Sky grabbed a fist full of hair and yanked her violently down to the ground. Then she sat in her chest. Danielle didn't stand a chance.

'Slap! Slap! Slap! Slap!'

Sky was drunk with anger.

" You little bitch!!!"

'Slap! Slap! Slap!'

Danielle's nose started bleeding and blood flew everywhere.

David jumped in and snatched his daughter into a bear hug and lifted her into the air.

Sky kicked wildly. "Let me go! Let me go!"

The crowd snapped pictures from their phones that were sure to be on the internet by the end of the day.

Out of nowhere, aunty Kathreen charged at Eric. "You little punk! This is your fault!"

Erick took off running and Kathreen tried her best to run after him. The crowd laughed at the sight.

David released his strong hold from Sky and he bent down in front of her.

"Sky! Sky!" he called out to her.

Sky still had Danielle in her sights. Danielle rolled on the ground bleeding and trying to gather herself.

Sky tried to force her way passed her father, but he grabbed her by her arms.

"Amber Sky! Calm down!... Calm down and look at me!"

The sound of her father screaming out both of her names snapped her out of her possessed daze. She looked at her father as he kneeled down in front of her. His expression was calm but she saw hurt in his eyes. The look on his face was able to hush the roaring anger that dwelled in her bosom.

"Are you okay Amber Sky?"

She nodded her head. "Yes Daddy."

"Good... I want you to stay right here."

David turned around and helped Danielle up off of the ground. Someone from the crowd rushed over with a towel and David took it and helped Danielle get her nose bleed under control. Once the blood stopped, he lead her over to where Sky was standing.

31

AMBER SKY
A.R. DASH

Sky balled her small hands into fist and her chest rose into the air. She let out a steamy breath through her nostrils and looked at Danielle. Danielle no longer looked like the sarcastic little witch that she was portraying to be. At the moment, she had just met a professional fighter.

David kneeled down in between the two girls and looked up at his daughter.

"Amber Sky. I know you are upset right now, and you probably do not want to hear much, but I need you to do something for me."

Sky stared down at her father. He was truly a weakness to her. She knew that he would walk through fire for her if he had to and she always tried to let him know that he would do the same.

She pushed all of her ill feelings to the side.

"What do you need me to do Daddy?"

David looked at Danielle.

"I need you to find the strength in yourself to forgive this young lady in front of you. Do you think that you could do that for me?"

Sky looked up at Danielle. David continued to speak.

"Remember Amber Sky, everybody deserves forgiveness because everybody makes mistakes."

His words were like magic that made any ill feelings of Sky's disappear. She looked up at Danielle with sincerity.

"I forgive you Danielle, and I truly apologize for putting my hands on you. Can you please forgive me?"

Danielle went from looking half scared to looking all the way baffled.

"Yea-yeah I forgive you. I-I-I hope that we can still be friends"

Sky stood there smiling but she wasn't sure if that was going to happen.

David looked at both girls with a burning seriousness in his eyes.

"I want to tell you two girls something and I don't want either of you to ever forget it?"

He had both of the girl's full attention.

"You two better always remember that you are females. God's greatest creation. It is because of you that the world goes round. You guys have something special, and that something is called Girl Power... Always remember that when you have Girl Power, nothing can get you down...You hear me?"

Both of the girls nodded their heads and then he repeated his statement, but this time Sky could feel the passion in his words.

"Don't you ever let anybody get you down, you have Girl Power!"

He looked at Sky.

"Now let me hear you say it."

Sky took a breath. "Can't nobody get me down because I have Girl Power."

David looked at Danielle. "Now you."

Danielle also took a breath. "Can't nobody get me down because I have Girl Power."

"Good." Said David.

Then he turned to Sky and presented the butterfly necklace to her and sadly, the next day he went out on his motorcycle and was involved in a terrible motorcycle accident with an eighteen wheel tractor trailer.

He died on impact.

Charlene packed up and moved away shortly after and Sky was forced to cut ties with her old life.

Not only did the accident take away Sky's loving father, but it also took away all of the happiness away from her family.

*

Now, here it was six years later, and Danielle was reaching out to her. She looked down at the phone on her bed, and then she picked it up.

"What the heck, I might as well give her a call. What could it hurt?"

CHAPTER
3.

Sky looked down at the Facebook request. She had a Facebook page but barely ever used it because she thought too much gossiping was involved with the whole social media thing. So instead of sending Danielle a message through Facebook, she decided to just give her a call.

Sky dialed the number, held her breath then put the phone to her ear.

It rang once. Sky's heart speeded up.

It rang twice. Sky thought about hanging up.

On the third ring a female answered in an uncertain tone.

"Hello?"

Sky forced herself to speak. *"Umm... Yeah... Umm... Danielle?"*

"Yes this is Danielle, whose calling?"

"It's me umm... It's sky."

Danielle's voice exploded through the phone.

"Oh my God! Sky? Are you serious? Is it really you."

"Yeah it's me. How are you doing Danielle?"

"Wow! I'm fine, I'm fine. I haven't heard from you in what, five-six years. How have you been? How's the family?"

A dis-spiriting vibration flowed through Sky and the excitement in her voice went dull.

I'm okay. I've been doing fine and I guess you can say the family's okay as well."

Her words were so weak that she didn't believe them herself. Danielle must have sensed her unease and didn't hesitate to speak on it.

AMBER SKY
A.R. DASH

"You don't sound fine. Is everything okay Sky? Sounds like something is really bothering you."

Danielle had no idea how right she was.

"No I'm okay, I'm okay. I'm just dealing with the issues of life, that's all."

"Uh-oh." Said Danielle. "Sounds like guy problems."

A vision of Josh jumped into Sky's head. He was indeed an issue but he was the least of Sky's worries.

"No Danielle, it's not that. I mean, I do have a few guy issues but there not that serious. Right now I'm just---"

Sky didn't know if opening up to Danielle was the right thing to do so she cut her words short. Danielle responded to her vibe.

"Listen, I know we haven't seen each other in a while, but I'm here to tell you, Sky you are a genuinely good person and I missed out on a chance to have you as a friend when we were younger. This is not the first time that I've thought about you, it's just the first time that I've had the heart to reach out to you. And now that I'm in touch with you, I plan to make good on that opportunity I messed up when we were kids-"

Sky's eyes watered up as Danielle continued to speak.

"You may not feel comfortable talking to me right now and you have good reason, but I've grown up Sky. I'm no longer that hot in the pants sixteen year old from the old neighborhood. I'm a lady now Sky; a married lady with a husband and two children. And more than that, Sky I'm ready to have that friendship with you that we should've had a long time ago. So you have my number and you can use it anytime you want. Even if I have no advice for you, I promise to at least be a good listener."

Sky felt a loving feeling that she hadn't felt since her father was alive. And the feeling told her that it was okay to open up a little. After all, Sky was a bit of a loner, so maybe a friend might do her some good.

Awww. That was so nice of you Danielle. You have no idea how much I needed the feeling that you just gave to me. Thank you for making my day."

"Come on Sky, Remember, Girl Power! Don't let them get you down-you got that Girl Power!"

Sky's chest tightened and she couldn't hold back the tears. Her voice choked up.

"Wow, you remember?"

"Are you kidding me? Of course I remember that. That was a valuable lesson that you father taught me and I've been living by that code ever since he said it to us. Heck, he's part of the reason that I straightened my act up, well that and the beating you put on me."

A feeling of awkwardness shot through Sky but Danielle laughed and brought ease to the moment.

"Sky girl, after that situation with Eric, I haven't even looked in the direction of somebody else's man. I went and found a man of my own. And when I tell you that I love him with all of my heart, I mean it. And if someone was to try to take him away from me, I would probably react the same way you did."

It finally registered that Danielle was married.

"You're really married with two children?"

"Yes girl, two kids and a husband to go along with them... Oh! Oh! Oh! Yeah! Listen, I've heard through the grapevine, and (Facebook) that your mother moved around a couple of

times and that you guys ended up living somewhere in Jersey City. Is that true?"

"Yeah we live in Jersey City. But did you really hear that on Facebook?"

"Yeah why?"

"Nah, because I really don't do the Facebook thing anymore. Too much gossip and drama for me."

"Oh, so that's why I haven't seen you on the Book huh?"

"Exactly."

"I feel you. I feel the same way and I only use it to show off pictures of my family, but listen, I have been working for the U.S. Post Office for the last four years and a manager position opened up here in Jersey City about eight months ago and I took it and moved out here."

"Really? Where at?"

"Well I live in the Greenville Section of Jersey City on J.F.K. and I work up in the Journal Square shopping area. Do you know where that is?"

"Yeah I know where that is. Wow! We're really neighbors."

Sky was about to jump up with excitement but sudden voices outside of her room door made her stiffen up. She sat as still as a board and focused her hearing to see who it was. Dustin's voice boomed with laughter. It sounded as if he had a house full of his friends.

Sky's mother had taken baby Lilly to the doctor and she'd taken Autumn along with her. Even though she was locked safely behind her room door, Sky found herself hoping that her mother would soon return. She was uncomfortable just knowing that she was alone in the house with a gang of creeps.

AMBER SKY
A.R. DASH

"Sky are you there?" asked Danielle.

"Yeah, yeah, I'm here. I'm sorry, I just heard my mother's no good fiancé and his friends and I kind of lost my train of thought."

"Your mother's new fiancé? Wow, I know it must've been hard for her to move on, the guy must be amazing if he's anything like your father was."

Sky almost threw up inside of her mouth

"Like my father? Are you kidding me? My mother's new fiancé is a straight up loser."

"Are you serious?"

"Very... and to make matters worse, she even has a daughter with him."

Danielle's voice rose ten notches.

"What!!! You have a new sister?"

The thought of baby Lilly brought a smile to Sky's heart.

"Yes I have a baby sister. Her name is Lilly. She's the most beautiful thing I've ever seen."

"Awww..."

"Yeah, that's why I need to fine me a job so I can take my siblings away from this house of horrors."

"What? Girl you need a job? I tell you, God sure does work in mysterious ways. This is perfect timing."

Sky didn't understand.

"Why do you say that?"

40

"Because... The Post Office is about to start doing some serious hiring in about a month or so and I can get you in for sure. That is if you don't mind being a mail lady?"

Sky jumped up off of the bed and squeezed the phone against the side of her face and prayed that this wasn't a joke.

"Are you serious? Because if you are, than heck, no I don't mind being a mail lady. Just tell me what I have to do to get started?"

"You don't have to do anything except for fill out the application, but like I said, the hiring doesn't start for another month or two."

Sky didn't care. She was with the wait. Then she heard a baby crying in Danielle's back round.

"Hold on for a minute Sky."

"Okay."

A split second later, Danielle came back to the phone.

"Sky let me call you another time, my son C.J. junior is crying for me. If you don't hear from me in the next couple of days it's only because I am busy, but don't worry, I got you okay?"

"Thank you so much, and Danielle, congratulations on the family."

"Thanks Sky... I've missed you so much and nothing will ever come between us again. I'll talk to you later."

"Okay."

Sky melted and fell backwards onto her bed and stared up at the ceiling.

"Thank you Lord. Thank you so much."

Sky was distracted from her thoughts a second time by the voices outside of her room. She reached up and touched her butterfly pendant then closed her eyes.

"Girl Power." She whispered.

The voices outside of her door drifted as if whoever was out there was leaving out of the house. Sky hoped so because the long conversation with Danielle had left her thirsty and she wanted to go to the kitchen to get some orange juice but she would die of dehydration before she left out of her room knowing that Dustin and his friends were out there.

The squeak of the front door opening gave Sky hope that they were leaving and then the closing of the door put her at ease. But she still wasn't one hundred percent certain that the coast was clear. So she walked over to her room door and eased it open about six inches. She heard no movement so she pulled the door open a little further. Then she poked her head out into the hallway and looked both ways. The hall was empty. She listened for about ten seconds then she tip-toed her bare feet into the hallway. She felt like a cat burglar in her own home.

The stinking smell of a cigarette filled her nose and she started breathing through her mouth because she hated the smell. With light steps, she eased down the distance of the hall and laughed at herself for having to be incognito just to get a glass of orange juice. Sky reached the end of the hall and as soon as she stepped foot into the kitchen her heart skipped a beat and she paused in mid-step. Dustin sat in silence at the kitchen table with a burning cigarette in his hand.

Her first thought was to turn around and to go back to her room but she didn't want to give him the pleasure of thinking that she was afraid of him because she wasn't. But she mentally kicked herself for having on the boy shorts and halter top instead of a pair of sweat pants and a long t-shirt. She justified her thought by telling herself that it wasn't her fault that he was a pervert.

Without acknowledging his presence, she walked over to the refrigerator and opened the door.

"How are you doing Amber Sky?"

Sky froze, and something inside of her felt like it was about to explode. She couldn't believe that he not only had the nerve to speak to her, but he also had the audacity to call her by both of her names. No one but her father was allowed to call her that and he was definitely not her father.

She spun around with an attitude to face him. His eyes rose from the lower portion of her body to her face and it sent a wave of disgust through her.

"Don't call me that! Don't you ever call me by that name again!"

Dustin put his hands up in mock surrender and his words came off as sincere.

"I'm sorry. I apologize. It won't ever happen again."

Sky rolled her eyes and turned back around to the refrigerator. She didn't see any orange juice so she slammed the door shut. She turned and was about to head back to her room but from the corner of her eye she caught a glance of the orange juice container sitting on the table next to Dustin's ashtray.

Her eyes cut towards Dustin.

"Is there anymore juice in there?"

He was so busy staring at her exposed legs and stomach to even realize that she was speaking to him. Even if he wanted to, he couldn't hide the lust in his eyes. Sky begged to God to tell her what the lesson was for him bringing such a low life to come into the lives of her family.

She snapped her fingers in his direction.

"Hello... Hello..."

Dustin came out of his perverted daze and looked up into Sky's face. For an uncomfortable second, he just looked into her eyes. Then in a slow motion he lifted his cigarette to his mouth and took a deep pull. The cloud of smoke rose in his face and he had to squint his eyes to see through it.

"I think there is some juice left in there, but I am not sure."

'Useless.' Sky thought.

She walked over to the table and snatched the container up into her hand and headed back to the sink. She was having a thought, and somehow it became words.

"You need to be ashamed of yourself. You are engaged to be married to my mother, and you are the father of my baby sister, but you still look at me like I'm some corner girl from the street. I'm about to be your step daughter-"

Sky felt her blood pressure starting to rise.

"What is wrong with you?"

Her words had to scratch Dustin's funny bone because a tiny smirk formed at the corner of his mouth.

Sky wanted to scream, but she caught herself because she didn't want to get into a shouting match with him.

"You know what Dustin, just forget it. Talking to you is only a waste of my breath."

She turned away from him again and grabbed a glass out of the dish rack and began to rinse it out with frustration. She just wanted to be out of his presence.

"It's not like that Sky. I swear to you it isn't. And if you would, can you please accept my apology for any ill feelings I

may have caused you... I completely understand how you feel and I want you to know that I only do the things I do because I've been trying to get your attention and I don't know of any other way of doing it. You're always so hard on me, and all I really wanted to do was talk to you."

Sky stopped rinsing out the glass. She pondered what he was saying and wondered if he was being serious or if he was being sarcastic. She had to admit to herself that she was definitely hard on him.

Sky was the type of person to give people the benefit of the doubt and maybe, just maybe, Dustin had seen the errors of his ways.

Sky sat the glass down next to the orange juice container and noticed that the container was open. She didn't see a glass on the table, which meant that Dustin had been drinking straight out of the carton. A disgusting chill shot through her body and she shivered knowing that she'd just dodged a bullet.

She no longer wanted any juice so she turned around and faced Dustin to see if she could read his intentions. He looked a hot mess. His would be five o'clock shadow was nothing more than a scruffy bushel of nappy facial hair; his eyes were heavy and blood shot red; his t-shirt was dingy and he looked like he hadn't slept in a couple of days. Or maybe he was just high on something.

Dustin smashed his cigarette out in the ashtray.

"You have no idea how bad I feel Sky. I truly feel terrible."

He sat up in his seat and rubbed his open palms on his knees. He looked around, took a deep breath and stared directly into Sky's face.

"Sky... Listen... I mean..."

He paused and scratched his head as if he was searching for the right words to say. A question mark began to grow inside of Sky's mind. She wanted to know what he was getting at. He began to speak again and Sky watched him closely.

"There is no other way for me to say what I have to say Sky."

He rose from his seat and took a step towards her.

"I love you mother Amber Sky and I would never do anything to hurt her."

"I told you not to call me that."

He took another step towards her.

Sky's heart started beating five times its normal pace. She didn't know what to think. All she knew was that she was alone with him and she didn't feel safe. She took a step back and bumped into the counter of the sink.

"Stay away from me Dustin."

He took another step.

"Sky, I am a man and you are a woman. It's okay for you to want me. There is nothing wrong with it because I want you also."

Suddenly a dark shadow came over his face.

"The only problem is, I don't think that you know how to respect a man the way you should, but don't worry, I'm about to teach you right now."

Sky's entire body was arrested in fear.

"You're crazy! You're sick!

He took another step and Sky screamed.

"Stay away from me!!!"

She tried to run passed him but Dustin grabbed her by the waist and pinned her against the counter. She screamed at the top of her lungs and tried to fight him off.

"Let me go! Get off of me! Let me go! Let me go!"

"Shut your damned mouth! Stop fighting me! You know you want this to happen!"

"Let me go! Get off of me! Let me go!!!"

Sky struggled, but the grip he had on her was too overpowering.

He applied force until she was bent backwards over the kitchen sink. Dustin was a possessed man. He spoke like a psycho who really believed that what he was doing was right.

"I've been waiting for this ever since the first day I saw you! And I could tell by the way you look at me that you've been waiting for this too!"

Sky squirmed wildly.

He got rougher. More aggressive.

"I remember how your mother use to fight like this until I set her straight."

"Stop!!!" she cried.

"That's right you little bitch! Fight your little heart out! It's time you learn how to respect the man of the house the way you're suppose too!"

Dustin let go of her arms and grabbed a hand full of her crotch.

She cried out.

"Noooo!!! Please Dustin! Let me goooo!!!"

"That's right little girl! Call out my name! Say it louder!"

With the arm that he'd let go of hers, she balled it into a little fist and swung uncontrollably. Her hits bounced off of him with no real effect. Dustin was a man on a mission. He tried to fit his hand down into the front of her shorts but he couldn't. The closed button on her shorts made them too tight for his big hand to squeeze into.

"Stoppp!!!" she cried.

He smelled like liquor and cigarettes. He jammed is hand down into her panties and the button popped and her shorts burst open. His rough ringers touched her pubic hair area and all she could do was scream.

"Noooo!!!"

She fought as hard as she could. He tried to kiss her on the mouth but she turned her head. There was a steak knife in the dish rack a little more than an arm's reach away. She stretched her arm out towards it. The tip of her finger was about two inches away.

Sky Scream.

"Ahhhh!!!"

But she could not reach the knife. She balled her little fist up again and swung a few more punches.

"Get off of me! Get off of me! Get off of me!"

It was a waste of energy. She felt herself getting weaker. She knew she didn't have much fight left in her. Her strength was all but gone. She had no choice but to accept what was about to happen. She let out one last cry before she lost her voice.

"Pleeease! Stoppp!!!"

Dustin mocked her.

"Pleeease! Stoppp!!!"

Then she gave up fighting.

Dustin let out a animal like grunt.

"Auuughhh!!!"

Tears trailed down Sky's face. She forced herself to think of a more beautiful moment in time. An image of her father popped into her head; he was smiling. She remembered he how he always told her to have Girl Power.

Dustin forced one of his fingers inside of her. Somehow, Sky was able to make her body shut down and go numb. She didn't want to feel what he was about to do to her. She just wanted it to all be over with.

Then she heard something coming from towards the living room. It sounded like keys. *'Mommy!'* she thought. Suddenly she felt hope. Dustin must've heard the same thing because he eased up the grip he had on her.

Sky found a new voice.

"Get off of me!!!"

With new strength she pushed him as hard as she could. He stumbled backwards but caught his balance. The sound of the keys got louder. Dustin moved with the swiftness of a bullet. He shot for the chair he was sitting in before he attacked Sky, but he wasn't fast enough. Autumn came running into the kitchen.

She stopped just as Dustin took his seat. Then she looked at her disheveled sister. Then she looked back at Dustin. He was trying to look calm but Autumns petrified face obviously knew something was wrong. Dustin shot her a threatening look.

There was never a time when Sky had been happier to see her sister. Sky bounced off of the kitchen counter and ran over to her sister and threw her arms around her.

"Where's Mommy?"

As soon as the words left Sky's mouth, her mother came walking into the kitchen carrying Lilly. She stopped dead in her tracks the same way Autumn did and took a quick glance at Dustin. Then she let her eyes burn on Sky. She looked her daughter up and down and it was clear that she was not pleased with the way Sky was dressed.

Sky leaped for her mother and cried out.

"Mom! Dustin just tried to ra---"

Charlene cut her off.

"Shut up Sky! I don't want to hear nothing you have to say!"

Roughly she handed Lilly to Autumn.

"Take her into my room!"

Autumn still looked like she was trying to figure out what was going on.

Charlene shouted. And gave Autumn a little shove.

"Do it now!"

Autumn scurried away and Sky approached her mother pleading.

"Mommy please, you have to listen to---"

"I don't want to hear it Sky! I've done told you a hundred times not to be walking around in my house dressed like that."

"But Mom-"

50

"But nothing Sky! I don't want to hear it!"

Dustin got up from his seat with a lit cigarette in his hand.

"I'm going to get the baby. But Charlene, you really need to have a talk with your daughter."

"Don't worry Dustin; I'm going to do a lot more than have a talk with her."

Dustin walked out of the kitchen and Sky's heart turned to stone. Charlene continued her verbal attack on her daughter.

The glare in Charlene's eyes was real.

"What did I tell you about dressing like that in my house Sky? Around my man?"

"Mom! He tried to rape me!"

"He did what?"

Charlene paused for a second and looked intensely into Sky's face.

"He tried to rape me Mom!"

"You little lying red heffa! Don't you dare lie on my man like that! He don't want you! Just look at you! You're dressed like a whore! And you want me to believe that he tried something with you, and not the other way around? Are you serious Sky?"

Sky stood there breathing heavily with her shorts burst open and the love for her mother dying. Then she pouted like a little girl.

"But Mommy he really tried to force himself on me."

The words didn't even reach Charlene.

AMBER SKY
A.R. DASH

"Since you don't like abiding by my rules, in my house, I think it's about time you start looking for somewhere else to live. I want you out of my house Sky."

Sky felt like a rope was being tightened around her neck. She dug deep inside of herself for air. Her vision was blurred by tears of painful rage. The feeling inside of her was one that she'd never felt. It had to be hate.

Charlene looked at Sky like she was a no good tramp and shook her head.

"Now go and put some decent clothes on and stop strutting around my house like you are some type of stripper or something. Have a little more respect for yourself and stop chasing attention. I raised you better than that."

Charlene left Sky standing there feeling naked. A part of Sky would never be the same again. She dragged her limp body into her room and closed the door behind her. Inside of her, a empty space was opening up.

Sky dropped down onto her bed in a lost daze. Unconsciously she reached up and started rubbing on the butterfly pendant. Through the room door she listened as her mother talked to the man who'd just violated her in the worst way.

Their voices were like acid eating away at Sky's body.

"I was just starting to worry about you Charlene. If you wouldn't have come home when you did, I probably would've come looking for you... Matter of fact, I'm sure I would have."

"Aww Dustin, that was so sweet. Did you really miss me?"

"I sure did. Now come here and give the man that loves you a kiss."

Sky felt like her soul was being tied into a knot.

52

She balled her body up into a fetal position and hugged her legs against her chest. The hot tears soaked her entire face as she pouted like a baby. She cried harder and harder and harder. And then she had a thought of herself reaching the knife and it mad her cry even harder because she knew that if she had gotten it into her possession, she would have used it.

CHAPTER 4.

AMBER SKY
A.R. DASH

Sky slept through the night and well into the next afternoon without anybody interrupting her. At about one thirty, the ringing of her cell phone woke her from her safe haven. She wiped the sleep out of her eyes then stretched and reached for her phone. Her boyfriend's name flashed across the screen.

Sky jerked up and sat Indian style on her bed. The phone rang again and then a third time, but Sky hesitated and cleared her throat. She didn't want to sound like a grown man when she answered. On the forth ring she took a quick breath and accepted the call.

Her voice was as innocent as a school girl's but in reality; Josh's call had awakened the woman inside of her.

"Hello?"

"Hello Sky? What's up sweetheart? How are you doing?"

His voice was as handsome as chocolate. Sky squirmed in her seat.

"I'm okay; just sitting in my room with my thoughts."

"Is that right?"

"Um-hmm."

"Well what were you thinking about, if you don't mind me asking?"

Sky hadn't really been thinking about anything because she was asleep. A thought of all of the madness going on in her house popped into her mind and she wanted to spill her heart out to him but she knew that that wasn't her reality with Josh. He was probably calling for one reason and one reason only, so she set aside her problem of the world and entered into the world of Josh.

"No I don't mind you asking me what I was thinking about because I was actually sitting here thinking about us."

55

"Oh really?"

"Um-hmm."

"Well, were they good thoughts or bad ones?"

"Ummmm…"

Sky decided to take advantage of the opportunity to have a serious conversation with him about a few things concerning their situationship.

"The thoughts I was having weren't good thoughts or bad thoughts. They were just-thoughts."

The tone of Josh's voice changed like he knew what she was about to say and he really wasn't interested in hearing it.

"Okay—what kind of thoughts Sky?"

"Relationship thoughts."

"Oh boy. Here we go. Let's do it. Go ahead Sky. Say what's on your mind."

Sky climbed off of her bed and her bare feet touched the cold wood floor. She walked over to the mirror and saw that she was still dressed in her clothes from yesterday. Her tight shorts were split open and no longer had a button. She looked away from the mirror and contemplated her next words carefully knowing that Josh always found a way to avoid when she talked about their relationship.

"Josh listen? I want you to hear me all the way out before you say anything okay?"

"Just say what you have to say."

"I will. Stop sounding so defensive."

"Psssst."

"Alright, alright, alright. I'll just say what I have to say."

Sky backed away from the mirror and sat on her bed.

"Josh... Lately I've been thinking a lot about you... I mean, about us. We've been seeing each other for over six months and I want to know where we're headed?"

"Where we're headed? What are you talking about, where we're headed?"

"I'm talking about us. We barely even know each other Josh."

"What! Are you serious? We do know each other."

"Oh yeah? Really? Well tell me something about me; anything. Tell me something that I like."

For a fraction of a second there was silence. Like Josh was thinking of something to say.

"Tell you something that you like. Well, I know for a fact that you like the way I make love to you."

"Josh!"

"What? I'm serious."

"No you're not... I'm serious... And that's exactly what I'm talking about. You don't know anything about me, and I definitely don't know anything about you."

The attitude returned to his voice.

"You don't know anything about me? Like what? What exactly do you want to know Sky?"

"Well for starters, I know you work for some big construction company and you're always traveling with them, and that's why we barely see each other. But I don't even know what the name of the company is."

"What the hell does any of that matter? The only thing that matters is that I love you and you love me. Now get dressed, I'm about to come and get you."

'Love' she thought. *'This guy must really take me for a fool.'*

"Josh stop avoiding this conversation."

"I'm not avoiding anything! Look, we've been together for six months and I buy you nice things, don't I?"

Sky wondered to herself *'what the hell do nice things have to do with anything?'*

"You do buy me nice stuff but--"

"But nothing. Let me hear you say it. Tell me that I am good to you."

She felt like a complete fool.

"You are good to me Josh but I want more than materialistic things."

"More than materialistic things. I do give you more than materialistic things. I give you my love. How many times have I told you that I love you? What? You think I just go around telling people that I love them? Matter of fact, you want me to tell you something, I will. I will tell you the same thing that I told you when we first started dating. I have been hurt so many times in my past that now I have a problem trusting people. That's why I'm such a private person... You were okay when I told you that back when we first me. What's changed since then? Oh, I get it; you don't remember me telling you that?"

"I do remember... But Josh, we've been seeing each other for over six months. How long do I have to wait before you start trusting me?"

Josh got offensive.

"Look girl!"

"Girl?"

"Yes, girl... I don't know who you think you are, or what you think gives you the right to be questioning me, but I am a thirty-one year old grown man with no ring on my finger. I don't even answer to my own mother. Why should I have to explain myself to a twenty-two year old little girl who lives at home with her mother and can't even come out to play unless she gets permission... Are you serious?"

The words stung Sky like a hard slap. She was reminded of how Dustin had called her a little girl. She sat there with the phone stuck to the side of her face in complete and utter shock. He'd never spoken to her like that before. She knew in her heart that the right thing to do was to hang up the phone and to never answer for him again. But she didn't. For some stupid reason, she continued to listen to what he had to say.

"Sky, are you there?" he said in a much calmer voice.

"Yeah I'm here."

"Listen, I only have a couple of days off of work before I have to be back on the road again. I'm sorry for my attitude but it's not you... it's this job. It really has me stressed out and tired. I was just hoping to get to spend some time with my lady before I have to be back to work. But if you don't want to spend any time with me then---"

"No Josh, it's not that—I do want to spend time with you but--"

"But what?"

Sky suppressed all of her feelings and bit the bullet.

"Nothing Josh... I'm just stressed out as well I guess and I'm taking it out on you, that's all. But you're right; it's not my place to question you like you are my child. Are you still coming to pick me up?"

"I don't know. I mean, do you trust me enough to be around me? Like you said, you don't know me and who knows, I could be a serial killer."

He meant it as a joke but Sky didn't find it funny. Somehow, she found the strength to sound unbothered.

"You know I trust you Josh."

On the inside, she felt like she was just as naive as her mother was. Josh's voice was as excited as it was when Sky first picked up the phone.

"Okay then. Stop wasting time interrogating me and start getting ready. I'll be there around four. That's about two hours from now."

"Wait Josh! Don't come at four. Come at six. I might have some cleaning to do."

As soon as the words left her mouth, she regretted saying them. He'd just called her a little girl and she'd just proven him right. But he didn't say anything.

"Six? Come on Sky. I haven't seen you in a while. I don't' know if I could wait that long."

He began to whine.

"I've missed you baby. I need to see you now."

His words were sweet to Sky's ears because at the moment she was in need of some serious affection.

She smiled from ear to ear.

"Boy, just be here at six."

"Okay, okay, I'll be there at six."

"Bye."

Josh hung up but Sky sat there for a few seconds holding the phone to her ear. Uncertainty crept into her mind. Maybe Josh was telling the truth about being a very private person; maybe she was paranoid for nothing; maybe her mind was playing tricks on her. Who was she to judge Josh. After all, this was the first time that she'd ever been involved with someone older than she was.

Sky sat the phone down and looked into the mirror at her reflection. The person in the mirror looked like a complete fool for trying to justify Josh's behavior. She shook her head at herself.

The phone call made her feel no better about her situation with Josh, but at least she was about to get away from the house of horrors for a while.

The thought of getting away brought ease to her mind. The only thing left to do now was to find something sexy to wear. She thought about having a good time and walked over to her closet and flipped through her wardrobe in search of an outfit for the night.

She spoke out loud to avoid her aggravating thoughts.

"I'll just question him about things later."

Thirty minutes sped by without her finding anything to wear. Frustration set in. she took a few articles of clothing still draping from hangers and flung them on her bed. She went to reach for some more hangers but unexpectedly, her room door burst open. Sky's heart hit her chest like it was trying to escape. Thoughts of what Dustin did rushed her mind. She dropped the clothes and spun around ready for whatever.

She saw Autumn.

Autumn eyes popped open and she stopped short.

"It's only me Sky. It's only me."

Sky put her hand on her chest to calm her nerves. She didn't want her sister to feel uncomfortable so she lied.

"It's okay Autumn. It's okay. You didn't scare me."

Sky bent down to gather the clothes from the floor. She made a mental note to get herself some type of weapon to keep at her bedside just in case.

"So what's up Autumn?"

"Nothing."

Her reply had no life to it and the look on her face wasn't the happy one that Sky was use to seeing. Then Autumn said something that caught Sky completely off guard.

"You were scared because you thought I was Dustin coming to do something to you, right?"

Sky felt a queasy feeling in her stomach and from her kneeling position she cocked her head to the side and looked at her sister inquisitively. Sky saw an innocent fear in Autumns eyes and it tore at her heart to know that her sister was afraid for her.

Slowly Sky got up and took a few steps towards her sister. Gently she held Autumn by the hand and led her over to the bed and they both sat down. Carefully Sky placed Autumn's warm hand in between both of hers. Autumn was Sky's miniature twin. Just a slimmer and younger version. The only really noticeable difference was Autumns light green eyes. Autumn appeared so harmless and fragile. Sky had an uncomfortable thought of Dustin trying the same thing on Autumn that he'd tried on her. A blazing fire that began at Sky's core quickly spread throughout every inch of her body.

If Dustin ever tried anything with Autumn, Sky wouldn't stop until either her or Dustin were in their grave.

It was a sensitive topic and Sky knew she had to choose her words wisely. She didn't want to scare her little sister or to put anything into her head.

"I'm not going to lie to you Autumn, I did think you were Dustin. But I wasn't really afraid; I was more or less getting prepared."

"Prepared for what? Did Dustin try to do something to you?"

Autumn may have been young but clearly she was far from stupid. There was no way that she hadn't heard all of the arguing in the house and put two and two together. Sky had to make a decision. She could either talk around the things going on inside of the house, or she could talk about them head on and let Autumn know that somebody had her back if she needed any kind of help.

"Yes Autumn, Dustin did try something with me. He tried to do something really bad to me and that's why I looked the way I did when you came running into the kitchen yesterday. And you want to know something?"

"What?"

"In all reality, you saved me."

Autumn smiled. *"I did?"*

"Yep. You did lil sis. Thank you so much for being my hero."

"You don't have to thank me Sky. We're sisters and we are supposed to protect each other from everything."

Goose bumps covered Sky's body.

"That's right Autumn. We're sisters and we are supposed to protect each other from everything?"

Autumn let go of Sky's hand and hugged her.

"I love you Sky. You're the best sister in the world."

"Thank you Autumn." Said Sky, and she hugged her sister back.

"I love you too lil sis. And I want you to know something; the same way you protected me, is the same way that I will protect you, from Dustin or anybody else. So always remember, if someone says or does anything to you that you don't think is right, you make sure you tell me okay?"

Autumn didn't answer. She just kept her arms locked around her sister. Sky backed out of the embrace and tried to look into her little sister's face but Autumn's eyes flickered away and she stared down at the floor.

"Autumn." Said Sky. *"Did you hear what I said to you?"*

Autumn continued to stare at the floor and she nodded her head up and down.

Sky spoke her name gently. *"Autumn."*

She looked up into Sky's face with the eyes of a lost puppy. Sky wondered what was wrong with her.

"Are you okay Autumn? Is something bothering you?"

Autumn looked back down at the floor. An unknown feeling invaded Sky. 'What if Dustin had tried—' She couldn't finish the thought.

"Autumn. Tell me what's bothering you. Did Dustin or somebody do something to you?"

Autumn jumped to her feet. *"No sky. No. Nobody did anything to me. It's nothing like that."*

"So why are you acting so strange?"

Autumn calmed down.

"Because Sky. You already know why. I don't like living here. We talk about it all of the time. And you always told me that you were going to become a nurse and we were going to move away from here. But now you're not going to be a nurse. How are we going to move now?"

Sky felt like someone was standing on her chest. All she could do was stare up into her sisters helpless eyes. She really didn't know what to say so she reached down and picked up Autumns hand again.

She had to say something.

"Autumn, you don't have to worry. I got us okay? No I am not going to be a nurse but guess what?" \She thought about Danielle. *"I am going to be a mail lady. And mail lady's make good money too. So I'm still going to be able to get us somewhere to live that's better than this is. Isn't that great?"*

Autumn's eyes lit up with joy.

"Really Sky? Really? Are you serious?"

Sky nodded her head and Autumn tackled her with a hug.

"You're the best sister in the world! I can't wait! I can't wait!"

Sky hugged Autumn honestly but on the inside she felt a little guilt. *'What if things didn't work out with Danielle, then what?'* Sky couldn't think about that right now. Right now she had to focus on comforting her sister.

She hugged Autumn a little longer and then she changed the subject.

"Now why did you come bursting in here like you was about to tell me that you hit the lottery or something?"

Autumn snatched back away from her sister.

"Oh yeah, I almost forgot. Mommy is about to take Dustin an all of us out to eat, and she told me to come and ask you if you wanted to come?"

The muscles in Sky's face tightened and Autumn didn't miss it.

"Please Sky, Please come with us."

Sky couldn't believe the nerve of her mother, but she also knew that her mother's bi-polar ways were partially to blame. She also knew that she wouldn't accept the offer if she was on her death bed and starving. As a matter of fact, her mother knew that even if they were in good standings, Sky would reject the offer. There was no way that she was about to watch her mother pay for, not only the children's food, but also for a worthless grown man's food. And even worse, Dustin had a habit of holding on to her mother's money so that when it came time to pay the bill, he could go into his pocket and pay to make it look like he was a decent man and footing the bill.

"I'm sorry Autumn, I'm going to have to pass on this one. I've already made plans."

Autumn's bright smile faded.

"Where are you going? Are you staying out all night?"

"Yeah I am, bit I'll be back first thing tomorrow morning."

Autumn whined. *"Do you have to go?"* She had the face of someone who was about to lose their best friend. Sky's heart sunk.

"I'll tell you what; how about I make a promise to you to spend the entire day with you tomorrow. Just the two of us; we

66

can hang out all day long and do whatever you want to do. How does that sound?"

The little girl's face lightened a little.

"Okay... but you promise right?"

"Yeah, I promise."

Sky still saw the hidden gloom behind Autumn's eyes and she couldn't stand to see her sister like that so she turned around slowly and began to gather her things from off of the floor. Sky looked up into the mirror and saw Autumn dragging her feet towards the door. Autumn grabbed the door knob and before she opened it, she turned to look at Sky one last time. Sky dropped her head. She couldn't look Autumn in the face. If she did, she would no doubt end up staying home. And Sky really wanted to get out of the house before she went crazy. Even if it was only for one night.

Sky waited until she was sure Autumn was gone before she stood up. She turned around and looked at the open doorway and thought that maybe Autumn was sad because her mother worked nights and more than likely, Autumn was going to be stuck babysitting Lilly. Lord only knows what Dustin was going to be doing while her mother was working. *'I really don't want to leave her in this house alone with Dustin.'* She thought. *'Hopefully he'll stay out with his loser friends all night like he usually does when my mom is at work.'*

Just as she was having the thought, Dustin slowly walked pass the open doorway. For a fraction of a second their eyes locked and the corner of his mouth curled into a sadistic smirk. It was a smirk that masked something sick. Chills of anger touched Sky's spine and she charged towards the door. She reached out and slammed the door so hard that a picture frame fell from her wall.

Fifteen minutes later, Sky was left in the house by herself. Although her mother didn't give her any orders, she decided to save herself the headache of hearing her mother's mouth later on so she went out into the living room and started cleaning the place from top to bottom.

For the next two hours or so, she cleaned relentlessly. Every corner of the house was spotless. The leather furniture was wiped clean; the T.V. screen had been dusted; she polished the hardwood floors; and she even fluffed the pillows. Then she went into the kitchen and washed every dish, organized everything into its proper place and sprayed the entire house down with a vanilla febreeze fragrance.

Even though she didn't like being forced to clean, she had to admit that she was pleased with her work. It put her in a good state of mind to know that her sister's didn't have to run around a filthy house.

Sky doubled checked the house and was certain that her mother would not be able to find anything to complain about. On her way to take a shower, she couldn't help but to laugh out loud knowing that her mother would somehow still be able to find something wrong.

"That lady has serious issues."

＊

Sky was in and out of the shower and dressed by six o'clock and Josh was parked out front waiting on her. Her mother and her siblings had not yet returned from there outing so Sky never got to find out for certain if her mother had to work or not. As she locked up the house, she said a silent prayer hoping that it was one of her mother's day's off.

Sky stood on the porch and looked both ways in search of Dustin's car. She didn't see it. Then she heard the beep of a horn and looked up the block and saw Josh standing outside of what looked like a brand new car. From where she stood, the car could've been a Lexus or something because it was really nice.

"Okay baby." She mumbled under her breath.

She approached Josh and he kissed her on the cheek as he held the door open for her.

"Um-hmm." She responded. *"Now you want to kiss me, but earlier I was just some little girl."*

Josh smiled handsomely. *"Come on baby... You know I was just messing with you."*

Sky got into the car and Josh closed the door. The new car smell filled her senses as she watched him get into the driver's seat. Swiftly she did a two second inspection of him without him even knowing it, and like always, his appearance was very pleasing to her.

Josh was a guy that kept himself well maintained. His dark skin was unblemished with a dazzling glow to it. His haircut, as well as his fresh shave was razor sharp, and his new outfit was so crispy, it looked like it had just come off the rack. Josh's fingernails were clean and manicured. Not the rough and calloused type that you would expect to see on a man who'd been working on a construction site for some years. Sky sat in silence but came to the conclusion that he had to be lying about his profession, and possible other things. She made a promise to herself to find out the true story behind the man that she trusted herself to for almost the past six months.

Josh maneuvered the vehicle into the traffic smoothly and then he looked over at Sky.

"You're beautiful. Is that a new dress? Because it fits your figure perfectly."

She sat there sheepishly and ate up his words. She knew that he was just trying to butter her up because of the sour conversation they had earlier, but she didn't care. She needed to be buttered up. He continued to compliment her and she hung on his every word. She didn't feel as though she was a fool for adoring his compliments because, like all girls, Sky needed to be told that she was beautiful, and she had the desire to have a good looking man at her side. Josh supplied that for her and she was going to enjoy it while it was there. Sky might not have known everything there was to know about him, but at least he didn't treat her the way Dustin treated her mother. And besides, she was committed to righting the wrongs of their relationship.

Josh took the usual routes of back streets and side blocks that led them to the highway and although Sky knew that he was headed straight for a motel room, she still hoped for something different.

She looked at him with a beaming smile on her face and spoke to him with an extra girly voice.

"So what do you have planned for us?"

There was a sudden change in his demeanor. He went from looking fresh and energetic to looking like he was suddenly tired. He took one of his hands off of the steering wheel and rubbed the back of his neck.

"I was hoping that we could grab something from Mc Donald's or somewhere and then get us a room. I'm exhausted. The company lost two of its laborers last week and I'm the one who ended up getting stuck with the extra load. For the past five days, I've been driving a two hundred pound jack hammer into a stadium of concrete."

Sky took a second look at his fingernails and he reached down and rubbed his lower back.

"My back is killing me baby, I swear it is."

He took his eyes off of the road just long enough to see how she was processing what he was saying but Sky kept her cool. She continued to look unbothered but she would have respected him more if he would have just come out and said that he wanted to have sex. She appeared cool, but on the inside she was screaming *'I'm tired of going to hotels and eating fast food! That's all we ever do! Why can't we go to a movie or to a restaurant like normal people?'*

She turned to him and smiled.

"Okay baby. Don't worry; I'll take care of you. When we get to the room, I will give you a back rub."

Then she faced forward and pulled down the passenger side visor. Some documents feel into her lap. Josh's neck snapped in her direction. She picked up the papers and saw that it was the registration card or something so she placed it into her lap and pulled out some strawberry lip gloss. She looked up and adjusted the mirror. Then she pursed out her lips and applied a light layer to her already shiny lips.

When she was done she blew herself a kiss and was about to put the documents back into the visor, but she saw a blue baby pacifier wedged into the back seat. Her heart skipped a beat and she jerked her head back and looked at it. Then she glared at Josh. *'He has a baby.'*

Josh looked towards her with a question mark expression.

"What?" he said in confusion.

Sky yanked her seatbelt off and stretched half of her body into the back of the car. Once she had the pacifier in her hand, she plopped her body back down into the seat and beamed her eyes at him.

"What?" he asked a second time.

Then he looked down into her hand as she raised it up into the air. She held the pacifier in between her thumb and index finger like it was something dirty.

"What is this?"

Josh's face froze and the car swerved, but he regained control quickly. Then he reached out and took the pacifier from her hand and tossed it back into the back seat.

"Oh that? That belongs to my nephew. I dropped him and my sister off just before I came to get you. I know that little brat is going crazy without that thing."

Sky replied with a mountain of doubt in her voice.

"Your sister? Your nephew? I didn't even know you had a sister."

Her words hung in the air for a second in between their silence and Sky could have sworn that his beautiful skin, that was just dry, was a little moist with sweat.

He kept his eyes on the road.

"I could have sworn that I told you about my sister Tina, and her son Anthony. Are you sure you don't remember me telling you that?" He didn't give her time to answer. *"Anyway, don't worry about it because you are going to get to meet them real soon."*

Sky couldn't believe her ears. She sat there shocked with joy. Maybe the talk on the phone earlier helped out more than she knew. But she still felt the need to hide her excitement while he spoke.

"I was going to wait until we get to the room to tell you, but what the hell, I might as well tell you now."

She stared at the side of his face as he drove and then he turned towards her and nudged her chin.

"Why is your face so tight? Cheer up."

She kept her little act going.

"Can you just say what you have to say Josh."

"Alright, alright, alright... sheesh... calm down already... Anyway, well after we got off the phone, I did some thinking that maybe you were right. We've been seeing each other for about

72

six months, and our relationship is kind of distant...I want us to be closer--"

Sky's heart grew in her chest, but she remained emotionless.

"—So, my nephew's birthday is coming up and he is going to be five. My sister is throwing him this huge party and my whole family is going to be there. I was wondering if you would like to come along with me? I mean... I think it's time that you met everyone."

Everything inside of Sky jumped at the same time.

"Really? Are you serious! You're going to introduce me to your family? Oh my God! Would I like to come? Yes!"

Sky's situationship had just become a real relationship. She leaped up and hugged him while he was still driving.

"Calm down girl. You're going to get us killed."

She let go of him and slapped him on his arm playfully.

"Why didn't you tell me? When is the party? I have to get me something to wear. Oh my God!"

"Don't worry about that. You know I'm going to make sure that you look nice. The party isn't until next month and when I drop you off in the morning, I'm going to give you the money so that you can get yourself something nice. But for now, you need to be thinking about what you can do when we get to this room to put a smile on my face like the one you have on yours."

She reached down and rubbed his lower back.

"Don't worry baby. I'm going to take good care of you okay?"

Josh smiled and Sky continued to talk about the party all the way until the got to the hotel room. Before she realized what was happening, she was wrapped up in the heat of Josh's passion. She no longer cared to ask him all of the questions she wanted to ask him until she found herself sitting up alone in the middle of the night.

Josh was in a coma like sleep and she laid on the opposite side of the bed with the sheets covering her up to her neck. An army of questions began stalking her mind. She turned around and switched positions so that she was facing Josh. He was really out like a light but even in his sleep, she couldn't deny his good looks. *'He can't be lying.'* She thought to herself. *'There's no way in the world that he came up with that whole story off of the top of his head like that. A sister? A nephew? A party? No way. But what if he is lying? What if that pacifier really belongs to a child of his?'* Her mind was working overtime. *'I have to believe him. There's no way that he would deny his own flesh and blood just to sleep with me. No man in his right mind would do that. And if they would, then that would make them a sick individual.'*

She gazed at Josh's face. Unease climbed into the pit of her stomach. A sudden urge to go to the bathroom caused her to flip the covers off of her body. She swung her feet to the floor and sat on the edge of the bed. Josh moved. She froze. She didn't want him to wake up, so she sat there for a second looking at him as he adjusted himself in his sleep. When he stopped moving, Sky eased up into a standing position. Then, on the other side of the room, on the night stand, Josh's cell phone lit up. It was on silent mode so it didn't make any noise.

Sky looked at it and wondered who could be calling him at four o'clock in the morning. With light steps, she crept around the bed and over to the nightstand. Flashing across the screen was the word *'Home'*. Sky took another look at Josh and thought *'Who does he live with that would be calling him at this hour? What if it's his girlfriend? Or worse, his wife?'*

She turned her attention back to the phone. *'Maybe it's important? Maybe I should answer it?'* The word *'Home'* flashed again. Sky balled up her fist and took a deep breath. If somebody snooped through her personal stuff she wouldn't like it so she couldn't see herself doing it to someone else. She exhaled hard then turned away from the phone and walked to the bathroom.

Sky eased into the bathroom and closed the door behind her. *'Something is not right.'* She thought, and then she turned on the cold water and splashed a little on her face. She looked up into the mirror but quickly turned away. She couldn't look at herself for long because she once again felt like a fool. After splashing some more water onto her face, she turned off the faucet and left the bathroom.

The phone was lighting up again. She walked over to it and stood there for a long minute with the angel of common sense asking her what she was waiting for. *'I have to do it.'* She tried to convince herself. Then she took the phone into her hand but put it back down just as quick as she picked it up. *'This is wrong.'* The devil was at work inside of her. And then she had a thought that put her mind a little at ease. *'Daddy always said that a skeleton that doesn't want to stay in the closet is always going to find its way out.'*

Josh moaned and Sky shot back over to her side of the bed and she sat down lightly. His sleepy voice cracked into the air.

"What's wrong baby? You can't sleep?"

"Um-Um." Was all that she could say.

With his soft hands, he reached over and pulled her close to him and wrapped her back into the passion of his arms. Josh began to make love to her and softly he whispered into her ear, all the things he probably thought she wanted to hear.

But the only thing wanted to know was, *'What is a child that is going to be five doing walking around sucking on a pacifier?'*

CHAPTER 5.

The sun was at its heights the next day when Josh was dropping Sky off. He stopped the car about four car lengths away from the house of horrors. Sky looked towards the house and saw a few of Dustin's friends crowded around the front porch. *'Why Lord, why?'*

She really didn't want to get out the car and she wished that she could stay with Josh, but that wasn't about to happen. Josh dug into his pocket and pulled out some money and handed her two new hundred dollar bills.

"Here you go baby. Get yourself something pretty to wear, and if you need something else, just let me know."

"Thank you Josh. I appreciate this, but when did you say the party was?"

He took thought.

"Umm. I'm not sure of the exact date, but I know for certain that it's during the last week of July. That's about four or five weeks from now. Next time I talk to my sister I'll find out."

"Okay. Again, thank you."

"No problem. You know I got you."

Josh leaned over and gave her a kiss. Sky took that as a signal that it was time to get out of the car. As soon as she closed the door, Josh pulled off. She looked after the car. *'Really?'* She was always told that a man was supposed to wait until the lady made it into the house safely before they pulled off. She guessed that Josh didn't get the memo.

As she watched the car, she noticed that he had is phone glued to his ear before he reached the corner. She couldn't help but to wonder if he was calling *'Home'*. She shook the thought and approached her house.

Three of Dustin's friends were crowded at the bottom of the steps blocking the pathway. She hoped that they would get up to clear the way for her so that she wouldn't have to speak to them, but that didn't happen.

There were three of them, but only one of them had the manners to get up. He had dreadlocks and Sky had never seen him before. The other two stayed seated on the steps looking at Sky with eyes filled with disrespectful lust. The sight of them brought a nasty taste to her mouth. Clearly they were friends of Dustin's.

The one sitting on the left looked like he may have been cute some time ago but now he looked worn out and tired from too many years in the street. As for the one on the right, there was just no hope. He was at least fifty pounds overweight, in desperate need of a haircut and his t-shirt, which was supposed to be white was a tannish beige color. Not to mention that he looked like he had a very unpleasant smell to himself. He sat there with a cigarette hanging from two of the driest pair of lips Sky had ever seen. They looked like corner boy rejects. She didn't even bother to look over at the one with the dreadlocks but she was certain that he had just as many defects as the other two.

Sky decided to try a civil approach.

"Excuse me guys, would you mind getting up so that I could get pass?"

They acted as if they didn't hear her. One stared at her breast and the other stared at her legs; violated couldn't even began to explain what she felt.

The fat one spoke without lifting his eyes up from her chest area.

"Who was that driving the nice car, your boyfriend?"

Sky responded with agitation.

"Can you two just let me pass?"

They ignored her again. The second guy, who was much skinnier, ogled at her legs, then he looked up at her.

"Are you bowlegged or is that a gap?... Put your legs together for me."

She couldn't believe his blatant disrespect. Her agitation turned into anger.

"What?"

For a split second, she found herself wishing that Josh would come running down the street to her rescue; quickly she realized that wasn't going to happen. And as usual, she was left to deal with the male chauvinistic pigs by herself. It was time to stoop down to their level.

She looked at them with eyes of fury.

"I don't know what's wrong with--"

"Hold on, hold on, hold on." Said the one with the dreadlocks.

Sky looked up into his face and the first thing she noticed was a long scar across his cheek. He looked at Sky with respect.

"Please excuse me, and please forgive them."

He turned to them with authority in both his eyes, and his voice.

"Can one of you tell me why yall are treating this young like that? She didn't do anything to either one of you."

He waved his hand like he was shooing away flies.

"Come on now, get up. Let the girl get through."

The skinny one didn't say a word. He just stood up and cleared the way. The fat one followed suit but he hid behind a phony laugh.

"We were just messing around with her, she knows it. We always kid with her."

Scarface must have been somehow offended because his voice darkened with base.

"You always kid around with her? Just look at her... does it look like she's having fun?"

They looked at Sky but neither one of them said anything. They both were standing and Sky had enough room to pass, but Sky's savior spoke again.

"Watch out, watch out. Just get out of her way so she can go up the stairs."

They came down off of the stairs without argument. Sky walked up the stairs without them saying anything else to her. She took out her keys and unlocked the door. Whoever the guy with the scar on his face was, continued to talk at the other two.

"What if she was you mother? Or your sister? Or your daughter? How would you feel if I treated one of them that way?"

Sky was truly grateful for him stepping up for her the way he did. It was the true act of a man. She hadn't known that type of protection since her father was alive. She entered the house and locked the door behind her. Then, out of nowhere, her wave of gratitude turned into a river of guilt. A situation that could have quickly gotten ugly was easily diffused by the stranger with the scar on his face.

She was about to turn around and open up the door to thank him, but the condition of the house caught her attention. The house that she slaved to clean, looked like it had been hit by a tornado. Her mouth fell open and slowly her head turned from one side of the room to the other. She saw crushed up beer cans, empty alcohol bottles, crushed up potato chip bags and all kinds of other garbage all over the floor.

Slowly she took a step forward. A flipped over ashtray with crushed up cigarette butts and ashes was spread all over the center rug. Furniture was pushed out of place and the house no longer smelled like vanilla. A musty funk lingered in the air. Sky saw a yellow puddle and it made her stomach turn. She didn't know if it was spilled beer, or if someone had been pissy drunk; Literally.

Nonchalantly, Charlene came strolling into the living room. She stopped short and threw her right hand up to her chest and made a surprised expression.

"Sky! You scared me. I didn't even know you were home."

Sky knew she was pretending, so she just looked at her with skepticism. It was the first time she was face to face with Charlene since the incident with Dustin.

Charlene turned her attention away from Sky and walked over to a chair that was turned onto its side and sat it upright. Then she spoke to Sky as if she was not at all bothered by the condition of the house.

"How was your night Sky? Did you enjoy yourself?"

Sky said nothing. She knew her mother well enough to know that she didn't care anything about how her night went. She was only being nice for two reasons: one was because she felt guilty about taking Dustin's side instead of hers and the other reason was because more than likely she wanted Sky to clean up the messy house. Sky despised her mother's bi-polar ways. She was like night and day. She would be nice and pretend that everything was okay for a day or so, and right after Sky did everything she was told to do, then Charlene would turn back into a evil witch.

Charlene picked up the ashtray from off of the center rug and smiled gleefully.

"I'm so glad that you're home. Now you can help me clean up this mess. Dustin and his friends had a little get together last

81

night, and as you can see--" Charlene waved her hand like she was show casing a new car on a show room floor. *"Things got a little out of control. But Dustin did tell me that everyone had fun. You should've been there."*

"What!" Shouted Sky.

Everything registered at the same time and a tiny flame in the pit of Sky's stomach, quickly consumed her entire body.

"You want me to help you do what? You must be out of your--"

She caught herself before she said something really disrespectful. She was tired of what was going on, but wisely, she re-thought her words.

"Mom. I'm not about to help you do anything. Didn't you see how clean this house was when you got back from eating yesterday? I slaved for hours just to that you wouldn't have too. Now look at this place!"

Sky didn't realize it, but her deep anger had her raising her voice.

"Why don't you tell Dustin and his no good friends to help you!"

Charlene continued to move around the room picking at the mess.

"Keep your voice down Sky. Dustin is back there in the room. He'll get upset if he hears you, and I don't feel like dealing with his non-sense."

Sky could have hit the roof.

"I don't give----"

For the second time, she had to catch herself.

"You're my mother and I try as hard as I can to respect you, but him! I don't care if he hears me or not! Actually, I want him to hear me! He needs to hear me! You aren't going to say anything to him."

Charlene stopped moving. The blank look on her face let Sky know that she had hit a nerve.

Sky softened her voice.

"Mommy, why do you let him run over you like this?"

Charlene's reply was a weak one. *"Girl please."* It sounded as if she was trying to convince herself and not Sky. *"He does not run over me. He and his friends had a little get together, that's all, and when I came in from work, Dustin was in the back sleep so I told him that I would clean or have you do it."*

"You told him what?"

Sky still hadn't moved from her spot.

"Why would you tell him something like that? It's not right! We are not his personal maids."

"I never said that we were his personal maids. I'm just saying that we are the women of the house so it's up to us to make sure that the house stays clean. Dustin is a man; he's just doing what men do."

The top of Sky's head felt like it was about to explode and her tongue grew a mind of its own.

"He's not a man. He's the furthest thing from a man that I have ever seen! And you!" Sky shook her head. *"It's just sad mom, it truly is."*

"Calm down Sky, calm down. Trust me, one day you will understand. One of these days, you're going to have a real man and not that play play stuff you are involved with. And when that day comes, then you will see."

The words cut like a cold knife through warm butter. Charlene had just taken a potshot at her and Sky had no choice but to shoot back.

She took about three steps in her mother's direction.

"First of all, I do have a real man. And he is ten times the man that Dustin will ever be. My man gets up every day and he goes to work; he drives his own car; he pays his own bills and he never expects me to foot the bill when we go out to eat. Plus he dresses nice and takes care of himself. Most importantly, he's not a creepy pervert."

Charlene's face was masked with sarcasm.

"Yeah Sky, whatever you say. Bit I just hope you don't think that you're fooling anyone except for yourself. Let's be real, you only see your so-called real man about three times a month. And that's only on the weekends. Do you ever think about that? Do you ever wonder what he's doing when he's not with you? ... Stop fooling yourself honey. You know as well as I do that Josh only comes around when he wants to get laid... So yeah, you really have yourself a bowl of cherries."

Sky's face screwed up because her mother was right.

"So what! So what I barely see him!"

Hearing herself repeat the words hurt more than hearing her mother say them.

"I much rather barely see him and wonder about what he is doing, then to always see him and know that he's not doing anything. You are disgusting for even being associated with him. I don't know how you could even lay down with him? He barely ever showers. That no good--"

She couldn't think of a word to describe Dustin.

The muscles in Charlene's face tightened. Clearly, Sky had hit her target. She charged at Sky like a bowling ball towards pins and she stopped with just enough space between them for her to point an angry finger into her daughter's face.

"You little heffa! Let me tell you something. I know what happened in that kitchen. Dustin told me how you tried to throw yourself at him, and how he would have slapped some sense into you if Autumn hadn't come in when she did... I told him that he should have knocked you head off of your shoulders. And that is exactly what he is going to do if you ever try something like that again."

Charlene's finger jabbed Sky's nose a few times and Sky didn't say anything, but she stood her ground.

Charlene shouted, and Sky felt little spittle's hitting her in the face. Her mother was so far gone that she saw thick spit forming at the corners of her mouth. It was nothing but wickedness in Charlene's eyes.

"And may the Good Lord be my witness. After he knocks some sense into you, I'm going to choke the life out of you with my bare hands."

Charlene took her finger and shoved it against sky's forehead and Sky's chest swelled up. Her mother had never been physical with her, but things were heading in that direction and Sky wasn't about to take much more than what her mother had just done.

It looked like Charlene had fumes coming out of her nostrils and she stood there like she wanted Sky to react.

"Now clean this house! I don't care who made the mess! I pay the bills in here, so I make the rules. And if you keep on smelling your hot Panties and acting like you can come and go as you please, one day really soon, you're going to put that key into the lock and it's not going to turn. And you are going to fine yourself sleeping right on the curb next to one of those cars you seem to like jumping in and out of so much!"

Sky stood as quiet as she possible could but on the inside, she was screaming with fury Charlene turned around with no regard and left her standing there fuming. She didn't turn around once, but if looks could kill, she would've saw that Sky's eyes were committing a triple homicide.

Her mother's room door slammed shut and the sudden sound of Dustin's echoing voice angered Sky more. It was like listening to chalk screech across a chalkboard.

Sky looked up towards the ceiling and closed her eyes. She realized that she had no win as long as she lived underneath her mother's roof. She blew out a hot breath and then looked around at the messy living room. A hurtful laugh escaped her soul and she forced her body to move into the direction of her room. She thought about Danielle and what it was going to be like once her friend got her the job at the Post Office.

Sky opened her room door and saw Autumn stretched out across her bed knocked out. She had on a pair of Sky's shorts and one of her sports bras. *'You better stay out of my stuff girl.'* Sky thought. Then she remembered her mother saying she was at work so that meant that Autumn was stuck with Lilly while Dustin entertained his no good friends. Sky felt a lump of pity for Autumn. The girl was thirteen going on thirty.

Sky closed her room door and remembered her own upbringing. She didn't have to deal with any of the headaches that Autumn was dealing with because their father was not only preparing them for the world; he was also protecting them from it.

Sky only wished she had paid more attention when he told her that it would be days like this; days when she would feel alone and like the whole world was against her; days when it seemed like nobody cared enough to even ask her how she was doing; and days when it felt as though the rain would just keep on falling. The way her father told her to handle days like this was to think about God, and to remember that he created her with the ability to carry any weight that he placed upon her shoulders. Not only the good, but that bad as well.

Sky rubbed her butterfly pendant. *'Daddy I know that you are watching over me, and I promise not to give up...If I don't have anything else, I know that I will always have Girl Power.'* Sky turned her attention to Autumn and made a promised to never again let the responsibility of their baby sister fall on her again.

She walked over to Autumn with sorrow in her heart and pulled the blanket back to cover the child. She smelled a stench... like pee, and then she looked down and saw that Autumn was lying in a wet circle. Sky shook her head. Autumn had let Lilly pee in the bed again. Usually she would be mad, but at the moment, there was no way that she was about to be upset with her sister. She wanted to wake her up, but Autumn was probably exhausted. Sky covered the child and then she took off her nice dress and put on some baggy sweatpants, an oversized sweat shirt and her Cinderella hat. It was time to make the doughnuts.

CHAPTER
6.

Two hours later, the living room was back in order and the house once again had the vanilla fragrance. The only thing left to be done was the kitchen. Sky walked across the living room to the bay style windows, opened all three, and enjoyed the mellow breeze that pushed pass the curtains. The light scent of vanilla floated throughout the house.

Sky turned away from the window and was about to head for the kitchen but the voices coming from outside caught her attention. Carefully, she eased one of her curtains back and did a one eyed peek. She saw her mother, Dustin and the three friends having an animated discussion.

Charlene sat at the top of the stairs with Dustin holding a can of beer sitting next to her. Baby Lilly was fast asleep in a baby chair in between them. And the three friends gathered at the bottom of the stairs. The two that was giving Sky the problem, also had open beer cans in their hands. *'Need to be ashamed'.* She thought. It was only a little after four o'clock in the afternoon and here they were already on their way to getting drunk. A ball of disgust swelled inside of Sky.

What she was seeing was one of the things she hated the most about moving to Jersey City. Back on Staten Island, it was very rare that she saw grown men standing around all day drinking and doing nothing. The men who were around in the neighborhood she lived in all had jobs, so with the precious free time they did get; they always spent it with their wives and children.

For the life of Sky, she could not figure out why her mother chose to surround herself with such people. Maybe it was because, after her father died, her mother had gone into a stage of depression and gained a lot of weight; maybe because of that, her mother probably felt insecure and like she couldn't get a better man than Dustin. But still, Sky thought it was the craziest thing in the world because when they were in Staten Island, Charlene talked about people like Dustin and his friends like they were cats and dogs. *'Now look at you?'* Sky thought as she eavesdropped from behind one of the curtains.

She started to wonder what life would be like if her father was still living but her thoughts were interrupted by the conversation that was taking place outside. Dustin and his friends were debating about what the best route was to take for a person to get the most out of public assistance. Sky laughed to herself as she tuned into Dustin's words.

"The easiest and fastest way to collect welfare is to go up to the welfare buildings dressed as a bum and pretend to be homeless; you don't really have to be homeless, but once they see you and you looked messed up and don't have anything, they'll put you in a shelter for six months. After you go through that little process, they find you a apartment and pay your rent for a whole year through a program they have called T.R.A."

Dustin looked at Charlene.

"That's where we went a couple of days ago and my process is already in motion. All I have to do now is check into the shelter once a day for the next six months and after that, here comes the checks. Charlene is going to pretend to be my landlord so they are going to be making the check out to her and we are going to be rolling in the doe. Right Carlene?"

Charlene nodded her head in agreement.

"That's right."

Sky couldn't believe her ears. Her mother was playing a part in scamming the welfare system. She didn't know if she was more ashamed or embarrassed to be her daughter.

Dustin's overweight friend quickly co-signed.

"Yep. That's the best way. And that's why tomorrow, first thing in the morning, I'm going to dress like a bum and walk right up in that welfare building like, What's Up?"

90

He started laughing and Sky laughed as well. But she wasn't laughing with him, she was laughing at him knowing it wouldn't be hard for him to pass as a bum.

Dustin's skinny friend took a sip of his beer.

"Yeah, that's one way to get over on the system, but what about when that year is up; Then what?" He took another swallow of the beer. *"See me; I know how to make the government give you a check every month for as long as you want it."*

Dustin looked sincerely interested. *"And how the hell are you gonna do that?"*

"All you have to do is go up to the welfare people and tell them that you live with someone and that that person is threatening to kick you out unless you pay them some kind of rent. If you do that, they can't deny you because they have something called general assistance that's available to everybody who is down on their luck. You'll get one hundred and forty dollars in cash with two hundred dollars' worth of food stamps to go along with it. The only catch is that you might have to do a little community service or something to keep the cash coming in. To me, that is the best way because that is how I get my check every month and I've been collecting for almost two years."

Sky's mind was completely boggled. *'He's actually taking pride in getting a hundred and forty dollars a month. How could anybody live off of that?'*

Then Charlene added her two cents to the conversation even though she had never been on any kind of public assistance in her life. Sky summed it up to be the reason why she sounded more like a person trying to fit in then a person making a valid point.

"Well I heard-" Started Charlene. *"-that it is better to just apply for something called Section Eight. Someone told me*

AMBER SKY
A.R. DASH

that Section Eight will pay like ninety percent of your bills and all you have to do is apply for it. "

Sky wondered if her mother felt as foolish as she looked. Then she realized that there was no way for her mother to look foolish when she was amongst a group of fools. Sky had heard enough. She turned to walk away but the guy with the scar on his face started talking and she wanted to see what non-sense he would add to the conversation.

Unexpectedly, his voice came off with a bit of charm to it.

"I think that public assistance should only be given to families who fall on hard times and not to a bunch of grown and physically able adults who are just looking for a free ride-"

Sky was impressed. Without him knowing it, he had her full attention.

"-People need to stop looking for the easy way out, there isn't one. The world would be a better place if people got up off of their lazy behinds and learned how to carry their own weight. But that's not going to happen. And the sad thing is that the government has no way of knowing the difference between the people who really need help and the one's just looking for a handout.-"

Dustin's listened and didn't interrupt but it was easy to see that he was dying to say something.

"-If you ask me, people should have more respect for themselves. They think that they're getting over but when they learn that welfare is not enough to survive off, and their troubles start mounting up, then they start pointing their fingers at any and everybody but themselves."

'Common sense?' Sky thought. She almost had to pinch herself to make sure she wasn't going crazy. She continued to listen to see if he had anything else to say but was quickly disappointer when Dustin took over the conversation.

Dustin got up off of his seat to speak his thoughts.

"So what you're standing here saying is that everybody on welfare has no respect for themselves?"

"No. that is not what I am saying at all. What I'm saying is that if you and your family have fallen on hard times, then by all means, you should turn to public assistance for help. But if there isn't anything wrong with you, than you need to go out and get a job. Stop leeching off of the system. That money comes from tax payers who get up and you out into the world to work hard every day."

Dustin's voice raised in defense.

"You're talking about a job like it is that easy to find"

A joy mingled inside of Sky as she watched the debate knowing that the guy wasn't holding back his thoughts about people like Dustin.

"Matter of fact-" said Dustin. "I'll tell you what; if you tell me where I can find a job, I swear, I'll leave right now to put in an application."

Sky stood behind the curtain as stiff as a board. She crossed her fingers in hopes that the friend would say something to make Dustin eat his words but he didn't have a chance to speak. Dustin must've thought that he said something fancy because he continued in a sarcastic tone.

"Just like I thought. You can't tell me where to find a job because you barely have one yourself. You work for a temp agency and half the time you don't get to go out to work yourself. And if you ask me, I think that is worse because you get up every day at 4:30 in the morning and go to that place just for them to tell you 'it's not enough work, come back tomorrow'. Ain't no way in the world I'm about to go through that."

AMBER SKY
A.R. DASH

Dustin gave the fat friend a head nod and a smirk as if he had just scored some type of points. Sky felt a sting of pain for Scarface, but when she looked at him, he didn't appear to be in the least bit bothered.

Scarface was extra calm but the words he spoke were sharp and vicious.

"You know something Dustin, you're right; I can't tell you where to find a job and I do barely have a job myself. But you know what I do have? What I do have is dignity; what I do have is pride; what I do have is self-respect. And because I have these things, I will not belittle myself by going up to the welfare office begging for a hand out. I'd rather continue to work hard, and if that doesn't work, I'll just work harder. Cause one things for sure and two things for certain; one, I am not starving, and two I know that things will get better. So in the meantime, the little jobs that I do come across are enough to hold me over until that time comes-"

Unconsciously, Sky smile and a giddy feeling dance around inside of her as she continued to listen.

"Do you know why I rather struggle Dustin? Because... Because I wasn't raised to live off of other people's hard work and sweat. I was always taught that when the going gets tough, the tough gets going."

Quickly Scarface cut his eyes towards Charlene and the he drank water from his water bottle.

Sky enjoyed the sight of the awkward silence. Her mother looked uncomfortable and she got up out of her seat and began to gather the baby's belongings. She avoided looking into anyone's face like she knew she was guilty of being the one that was being liver off of.

Sky couldn't contain herself. She jumped up and threw her hand into the air and pulled it down like she was pulling a lever of a slot machine. *"Yes!"*

AMBER SKY
A.R. DASH

Her arm got caught in the curtain and it caused everyone to look up at the window. Sky ducked down to the floor and covered her mouth and giggled.

They continued their conversation without much thought and Sky heard the guy with the scar on his face ask her mother if he could use her bathroom. Charlene told him how to get there and Sky peeked up to see him coming up the stairs. Sky jumped up and made a dash for the kitchen and darted over to the sink. It was filled with dirty dishes and bubbly water.

She stood over the sudsy water dressed in her oversized clothes and she put on a stone face and prepared herself for anything. It didn't matter if the guy with the scar seemed to have common sense. At the end of the day, he was still one of Dustin's friends. It could have been just because he was in front of others that he was portraying to be a nice person.

The creek of the front door opening made Sky focus her attention on the dishes in front of her. She heard footsteps walking across the hardwood floor and she rolled her sleeves up and dipped her arms into the suds. The water was luke warm. Her hands swam through the heated water until she located a sponge. Then she picked up spaghetti stained plate and began to scrub.

Seconds later, the footsteps stopped and Sky got the feeling that she was being watched, but she didn't turn around. Three seconds of the uncomfortable vibe passed and she could no longer resist the urge to look up. Her intensions were to let the stranger know how rude it was to stare at people, but she never got to say a word.

He stood in the doorway looking at her. She peered up into his eyes and something inside of her surged, and she fell lost in his gaze. For what felt like a lifetime of seconds, they were like two deer caught in each other's headlights. Nothing existed but them. The burning curiosity in his eyes was inviting and as warm as the soapy water. It felt like he was looking into her mind and soul; like his eyes was piercing her heart and reading the most personal and intimate pages of her life story. Their eyes spoke a language of no words.

But it was just a simple stare.

Sky found the strength to bring her thoughts back to reality and pulled her eyes away from him. She looked down at the suds and then he spoke. He spoke words that sounded like they were from his heart; words that Sky would remember for the rest of her life.

His voice was gentle.

"You are the most beautiful woman I've ever seen in my life-"

Sky couldn't help but to look up and give him her attention.

"-If I had it my way, I'd run away with you right now and take you far away from this place; and take you somewhere where the world isn't so ugly; I don't know how I would do it, but each and every day, I'd figure out a way to make you smile."

Slowly he backed out of the doorway and disappeared without even going to the bathroom. Sky looked after him. The doorway was empty and the front door closed. What he said was the sweetest thing she ever heard. She stood at odds with herself. Part of her didn't want to believe that one of Dustin's friends was able to make her smile on the inside, but the other part of her couldn't deny that it had just happened. Sky went back to washing the dishes and feeling like Cinderella. But for the first time in a while, her soul didn't feel heavy.

CHAPTER 7.

His name was Chance...

Dustin's friend with the neat dreadlocks and the scar on his face and the beautiful words in his heart, name was Chance. Sky sat in the back of a bus on her way to the Journal Square shopping area to meet up with Danielle at the Post Office. Thoughts of Chance occupied her mind.

An entire week had gone by since they stood in the kitchen lost in each other's eyes and she was thinking about him because she hadn't seen him come by the house since. She didn't care that she was thinking about him. She felt a smile touch her face and she mumbled. *'Why are you thinking about him Sky?'* The lady sitting next to her looked at her and raised a eyebrow. Sky dropped the smile from her face and gave the lady a *mind your own business* glare. The lady looked away.

Sky's phone vibrated and she looked down. It was a text from Danielle. *'Are you close?'* Sky texted back. *'I'm about fifteen minutes away'* Danielle sent back a smiley emoji and it warmed Sky's heart.

Danielle called Sky earlier in the day and told her that the hiring would be starting in the next three to four weeks and she wanted Sky to come and fill out the application so that she could make sure it found its way to the top of the pile.

Sky was very thankful for Danielle. She had told Autumn everything that was going on and how Danielle was the one making it happen. But Sky did have some doubt because the reality was that her and Danielle hadn't seen one another in years, and the last memory they shared was the fight they had. Sky didn't know how she was going to approach Danielle, but she knew she had to do it.

The bus traveled at a moderate speed and Sky sat with a piece of mind. At every turn of her head she saw people out and about. Some people were outside just enjoying the summer weather, and others moved at a faster pace like they were out handling business. In any event, as she gazed out of the window at the busy world she realized that it didn't matter

what problems she had; the world was going to continue on
with or without her.

Sky admired all of the people just for having the courage to
face life; unlike herself. She had allowed her mother and the
house of horrors to steal her joy. All she did now a days was
sit locked up in her room. But that was about to change. Sky
was on her way to put in the application that would not only
change her life, but she would also be able to give her siblings
the life they weren't getting from Dustin and their mother.

Sky turned her attention to a young couple that sat a few
seats up from her. Neither one of them looked over twenty-
two. They were in the midst of a quiet but heated discussion.
Sky couldn't help but to be nosy.

Their argument had something to do with the girl not
coming home the night before. Mentally Sky felt pity for the
guy and she shook her head. Sky would love to have a man to
come home to and to call her own. *'Some people take
advantage of the wrong things in life.'*

The loud cries of an infant caused her to look into another
direction. Then the smell of a dirty diaper filled the air. A girl
about Sky's age held the crying baby on her lap. She had no
carriage and no bag. All she had was a almost empty bottle.
She looked like she didn't know what to do. She tried to stick
the bottle into the baby's mouth but the baby swatted it away.
The girl's face frowned in agitation and she sat the baby
upright and bounced the child on her knee roughly.

The smell of the diaper grew stronger and some of the
passengers mumbled under their breath while others screwed
up their faces. Every time the bus stopped to let someone off
or to pick someone up, the young mother huffed and puffed
like she was about to cry herself.

Sky raised her head to the heavens and thanked the Lord
for not laying such a burdensome fate upon her.

AMBER SKY
A.R. DASH

As the bus ran its route, Sky looked out the window and her mind drifted back to the guy named Chance. She wondered who he was. His style of dress wasn't immaculate, but it was far better than the group of people he hung out with. The scar across his check made him appear a little standoffish, but he still didn't fit in with Dustin and the others. Something made him stick out like a sore thumb. Maybe it was because the company he kept was immature and full of mommy issues and he seemed to have a manly confidence about himself.

He acted as if he had a reason to walk with his head held high. Sky wondered what that reason was. She'd only seen him once, but he managed to leave a very strong first impression. *'But why am I thinking about him?'* She asked herself. But for the life of her, she could not figure it out. *'So what he was able to melt my heart; so what he appeared to be different from his friends; so what he defended me and didn't disrespect me the way that everyone else does.* The reality of the situation was that no matter how she looked at it, Chance was still a friend of Dustin's. And that alone spoke volumes.

Sky was about three minutes away from the Post Office and she caught herself replaying Chance's words. *'You are the most beautiful woman I've ever seen in my life; if I had it my way, I'd run away with you right now and take you somewhere where the world isn't so ugly; I don't know how I'd do it, but each and every day, I'd figure out a way to make you smile'.* Sky would love for someone to make her smile everyday.

Suddenly it hit her like a sack of bricks. Chance's approach was as different as it was cute, but all the same, it was an attempt at her womanhood. He could try to sugar coat it anyway he wanted too, bit in the end, he as just another guy trying to get her into bed. The last thought she had of him wasn't a good one.

Sky's stop was the next one so she reached over and pressed the yellow strip to signal the bus driver. A ding sounded, a sign at the front of the bus lit up and the bus spoke *'Stop Requested'.* The driver pulled over and the doors opened up. *'Please watch your step upon entering and exiting the bus'.* Sky stood up and as she walked down the aisle, the young mother with the smelly baby huffed at her in annoyance. Sky turned towards the girl and was met with a dirty look. The girl looked like she wanted to push Sky off of the bus. Sky laughed to herself. And knowing that the girl was in a rush to get somewhere where she could change the baby, she purposely stopped next to the bus driver before getting off of the bus.

Sky leaned into the bus driver and pointed at the building that was obviously the Post Office.

"Excuse me Sir? Is that the Post Office over there?"

"Yes ma'am it is."

"Thank you."

Sky turned around and saw the girls face flame up in anger. She was tempted to stick her tongue out at the girl but she just smirked and got off of the bus. *'I'm bad'* thought Sky.

Sky stepped onto the curb and was greeted by a warm summer breeze. For no reason, she shielded her eyes and looked up at the sky. There were no clouds, just a lonely sun shining in all of its glory.

People walked in both directions. The traffic was light and she walked towards the building nervously. Approaching the building gave her a feeling like she was approaching a huge mountain. The entrance was at the end of a parking lot and Sky took careful steps across the pavement. A fleet of mail carrying trucks were both to her left and to her right. She walked pass the mail trucks and gave each one of them an equal amount of admiration. She even imagined herself behind the wheel of one of them one day.

The possibility of being a part of something as big as the United States Postal Service filled her with a shock of courage and even helped to calm her nerves a little. She held her head high and poked her chest out and walked up to the entrance of the building with confidence.

She was about to reach for the door handle but a young man dressed to deliver mail pushed the door open and almost hit her.

"Oh, excuse me... I didn't see you. I apologize."

Sky thought he was handsome.

"It's okay." She replied.

He nodded his head.

"You have a nice day." And he went about his business.

Sky stepped inside and before the door closed behind her the thrilling feeling disappeared and was replaced with an invasion of out of control butterflies in her stomach. The Post Office was as busy as a stock exchange room and up until this very moment, Sky hadn't really considered how big of a step in life she was taking. Filling out the application was equivalent to crossing over from adolescence to adulthood. If she could land this job, so much would change. She would no longer have to subject herself to living as her mother's puppet. She could save up enough money for her own apartment and she would no longer have to deal with the sexual harassment from Dustin and his loser friends.

Somehow, she was going to convince her mother to let her bring her siblings along with her. Sky relished in the thought of possibly being able to get her thirteen year old sister away from men she knew to be predators.

She could not afford to be nervous, so she called on God for strength. *'Gimme the strength I need Lord'.* And then she walked through the Post Office confident that she was covered in the armor of God.

Sky moved around the crowd and looked behind the counter in search of Danielle. Hopefully she didn't look too much different. For a second, all of the Post Office workers looked the same because they were dressed the same and each of them moved about the facility with diligence as they carried out their duties.

Sky stopped in the middle of the room and looked around and then located Danielle behind the counter talking to a customer. Danielle did indeed look a little different. She had the same face, but she appeared to have gained a considerable amount of weight. Maybe it was due to her pregnancies.

Danielle must've sensed that she was being watched because her round face looked up and locked eyes with Sky. Danielle's face lit up like a Christmas tree. She threw her hand into the air and waved hello to Sky. Timidly, Sky returned the greeting. Danielle put a finger in the air to indicate that she would be with her in a minute.

When Danielle was done helping the customer, she got another Postal worker to fill in for her and she disappeared out of sight. A couple of moments later, she came out from behind a door that had a sign *'Authorized Personnel Only'*.

Danielle carried a white document in her hand. Sky assumed that it was her application.

Danielle walked up to her with a lively voice.

"Hey girl! Look at you. Still looking awesome."

They embraced each other and Sky felt the love in Danielle's hug.

"For a minute I started to think you didn't want the job." Joked Danielle.

Sky looked at her in all seriousness.

"Girl not even Anthrax could have kept me away from this building."

Danielle laughed. *"Don't say that too loud. You might start a riot."*

They slapped each other a hi-five and Danielle caught Sky's hand and looked directly into her eyes.

"That's the attitude I was hoping you came up in here with. But listen, I have about fifteen minutes before my break, then I am going to help you fill out this application and we are going to go down the street to the sandwich to have a talk."

Sky nodded her head in respect as if Danielle was somehow her elder.

She handed Sky the documents. *"In the meantime, you can go over it yourself."*

Sky took the application and Danielle went back to her post.

Butterflies controlled Sky as she looked over the application but she couldn't help but to look up at her childhood friend. The sight of Danielle handling her duties captivated Sky and Sky could tell by the vibe she got from Danielle that she was probably in for a grown up talking too.

Sky prepared herself mentally because a stern talking too might be just what she needed to calm some of the troublesome thoughts she'd been having.

Danielle wrapped up her duties and sky looked on with a touch of envy. Danielle appeared to have grown so much. They were the same age, but only in years. As far as life was concerned, Danielle had her beat by a land slide. Danielle had so much going on; she was married; she had two children; she had a full time job and a house and a car note… Sky wondered to herself why life hadn't been as pleasant to her.

Danielle walked over to Sky, and together they filled out the application. A few minutes later, they were seated in front of each other at the sandwich shop down the street.

A turkey and cheese hero with everything on it, including extra oil and vinegar, sat untouched on the table in between them. They did a quick catch up and the more Sky got to re-know Danielle, the heavier her burdens got.

"So what's up Sky? What's going on in your life?"

"Nothing." Replied Sky in a dry tone. *"Nothing at all."*

Sky's hands were folded on top of the table and Danielle reached over the sandwich and placed a caring touch of top of Sky's.

"Something is wrong. I can tell by the distant look in your eyes and the sadness on your face. You look like you are living in a world of hurt. I know we haven't seen each other in a while, but I am here for you. Talk to me Sky, you can't keep you problems bottled up like that. It's not healthy."

Sky looked up into Danielle's face and saw that the concern was real. All of the things going on in Sky's life flashed through her mind at the same time and she was about to say something, but her words were stuck in her throat. All she could do was stare into her friends eyes. Sky felt empty on the inside. The world was draining her of her love.

Danielle squeezed her hand lovingly.

"Talk to me Sky."

"I don't know what to say."

"Say anything. Trust me; it will make you feel better."

"I doubt that seriously."

She shook Sky's hands. *"Don't doubt it Sky, try it. Just let it out."*

Sky continued to look into her friends face. Then she got mad at her thoughts and just let them out.

"First off my mother got me kicked out of nursing school, then her fiancé tried to rape me. Because of that, my mother has been threatening to kick me out of her house... Let's see, next I found a baby's pacifier in my boyfriend's back seat, he claims it's his nephews. Then umm... What else."

Danielle's mouth fell open before Sky could finish.

"Oh yeah, how can I forget. One of my mother's fiancé's friends said I was the most beautiful woman he's ever seen and he wants to marry me and take me away to his magical kingdom."

Sky felt like she let out some steam. Danielle sat there dumbfounded. Clearly she wasn't prepared for the kind of bombs Sky was dropping on her.

"You're mother's fiancé tried to---Your mother--- You found a---"

Danielle could not complete a sentence. Sky sat there emotionless. Danielle's eyes watered as if she wanted to cry for her. She got up out of her seat and walked over to Sky's side of the table and wrapped her arms around her tightly. Sky rested her head comfortably on Danielle's chest. The Indian man behind the register looked on with curiosity.

Danielle spoke softly.

"Your mother's fiancé is sick. Are you okay?"

Sky nodded her head and Danielle continued to embrace her.

"My God Sky, I didn't know it was this bad."

Sky's heart felt like stone, and for a long second, she hated life.

She pulled back away from Danielle with tears in her eyes but wiped them before they fell.

"I'm okay, I'm okay. I mean, what don't kill you makes you stronger right?"

Sky felt like she'd just shared a world of embarrassing secrets and she made a weak smile. Danielle reached out and gripped onto Sky's shoulders.

"Why didn't you tell your mother what really happened?"

"I tried too but she didn't believe me. It's like he has a hold on her mind or something. He told her that I tried to force myself on him and she believed him."

Danielle took a step backwards.

"What! Are you serious? What is wrong with her?"

Sadly Sky shook her head from side to side. More tears fell and she wiped them away with the palms of her hands. Danielle looked distant for a second like she was taking deep thought and was letting everything register. She helped Sky dry her wet face and then she took her seat on the opposite side of the table.

Danielle began to speak in a serious tone.

"We have to get you out of that house. Look, I have some emergency money in my account that you can have. My husband C.J. won't---"

"No... No...NO..." Sky protested. *"I'm alright. I can handle everything on my own. I just have to get a job."*

AMBER SKY
A.R. DASH

"Sky please... Just take the money. Don't let foolish pride block your blessing. It's about twenty-one hundred dollars and it will get you off of the ground until you start working at the Post Office with me. You don't even have to pay me back. But what you do have to do is get out of that house."

Danielle's offer was a good one but Sky couldn't see herself taking food out of Danielle's family mouth.

"Trust me Danielle, I can put up with this until I get the job." She shrugged her shoulders unconvincingly. *"I've been doing it this long, right?"*

She didn't even sound like she believed herself and Danielle didn't seem like she was going to take no for an answer.

"Sky! What do you mean you can put up with this? Are you crazy?"

The words sat in between their silence for a long second before Danielle began to talk with more authority.

"You have to push your foolish pride to the side Sky. Seriously! It doesn't matter that you've been able to handle the situation for this long. 'The situation' as you call it, is crazy. And you need out of it."

Hearing the reality hurt.

"It's time to get real Sky; your life is in danger. I'm only telling you this because I'm your friend. I'm only trying to help you because I care. Sky, Girl Power, remember."

Sky's eyes welled up again. She knew her friend meant well and she really wanted to accept the money but she just couldn't take food off of Danielle's table. And Sky didn't consider herself a charity case. The words she overheard Chance sat to Dustin replayed in her head. *A grown adult shouldn't reach for handouts if they are fully capable of working and helping themselves'* She couldn't believe that she was again reciting one of his quotes. A smile crawled onto her face and it caught Danielle by surprise.

"Why the heck are you smiling? What in the world are you thinking about that has you sitting here grinning?"

An image of Chance standing in the kitchen doorway popped into her head and she smiled harder. She forced the thought of Chance from her mind and her smile faded.

"I'm not thinking about nothing. I'm just going crazy, that's all. But really Danielle, how about this? If anything else happens, I promise to take you up on your offer. I'll even come to you for the money. Okay?"

Danielle looked like she wanted to argue Sky's decision but must've realized that it was of no use, so in a meek voice she agreed.

"Alright Sky. But you have to give me you word."

"You have my word. I promise."

"Good, and remember, if you need help in any way, I'm here for you."

Sky closed her eyes and nodded her head in gratitude. Danielle interrupted her thoughts.

"But totally off subject. What in Gods good name were you smiling about a minute ago?"

Sky tried to fight the urge to smile again but couldn't resist and her mouth curled at the corner. For the third time in a matter of minutes, a thought of Chance caused her face to light up. This time the silliness rubbed off on Danielle and she also grinned.

"What is wrong with you girl?"

Suddenly, as if a light bulb had gone off inside of her, Danielle jumped up out of her seat and covered her mouth with one hand and pointed a finger at Sky with the other.

"I got it... I got it...I know why you're smiling."

The outburst caused the cashier and a new customer to look in their direction, but Danielle didn't care.

"It's that guy that said he was going to take you to his magical kingdom... You like him!"

Sky grinned from ear to ear and she suddenly felt naked.

"What are you talking about?"

"I knew it! I knew it!"

Danielle dropped back down into her seat. She leaned up on the table with both of her elbows and spoke in a hushed voice.

"I want to know everything. Who is he? Does the guy that you're in a relationship with know about him?"

Sky's body tensed up at the mention of Josh. It wasn't the same feeling she got when she thought of Chance.

"No, the guy that I'm seeing doesn't know about him because there's nothing to know. And by the way, I'm not in a relationship; I'm in what you call a situationship, but Heaven only knows how bad I want this thing with Josh to be real."

Danielle calmed down. *"That's right, you did say something a while ago about him trying to hide his child from you."*

"No. He didn't try to hide his child. I found a pacifier in the back seat of his car and he claimed that it belonged to his nephew."

"And you don't believe him?"

"I mean... I want to believe him but for some reason, things aren't sitting right with me."

Danielle sat back in her seat. Doubt crawled onto her face.

"I don't know Sky. That's a rather strong accusation. A man would have to be the lowest of the low to deny his child. And to be perfectly honest, I just can't see a man doing that. When I think about my husband C.J. and how attached he is to our children-" Danielle paused for affect and Sky saw nothing but happiness in her friends face. *"-C.J. wouldn't let Jesus Christ himself come between him and them children, much less a female. He won't even let the kids stay at his mother's house for the weekend if he's not staying there with them."*

Sky hung on to Danielle's every word and felt another pinch of envy. Danielle's husband was the type of man she yearned for.

"I hear you Danielle, but not all men are like your husband. If they were, Josh and I would be married and living happily ever after. But that's not the case and some people just have to accept the fact that they have to go through life without ever experiencing true love."

"That's not true Sky. There's a love out there for everybody. The thing is, you have to stop playing games with yourself and eliminate all of those people, places and things from your life that are not good for you. It might hurt for a minute, and you might be lonely for a while, but that's the only way to make room the better things that is sure to come."

Sky sat mute. Danielle made complete sense, and at that moment, Sky made a promise to be true to herself.

"Well he said that his nephew is having a birthday party soon, and he even gave me the money to buy a dress. If everything goes right with this, then I stick it out a little longer with him. But if even the smallest thing goes wrong, I'm getting out of this situationship and making room for a real love."

"That's my girl. Just wait until the party to see what's going on and if anything is fishy, just drop the dirt bag."

Sky's face brightened.

"That's exactly what I am going to do. But forget about him, I hope in the next couple of weeks to be somebody's mail lady."

"Don't worry about that; that's in the bag, you have my word."

They moved to give each other a hi-five, and they spoke at the exact same time.

"Girl Power."

CHAPTER
8.

For the entire bus ride back to the house of horrors, Sky paid little attention to the things that went on around her. She was too busy thinking about what life was going to be like once she got the job at the Post Office. By the time her bus ride ended, she'd instilled all of her faith and trust in Danielle. There were no longer any ifs, ands or buts about her future. She was completely confident that she was getting the job. Her dad had told her that true faith is to believe the thing you desire is already yours. So in her mind she was already an employee of the U.S. Post Office. She was ultra-excited, but as she approached the house of horrors, the excitement quickly faded.

Sky hoped that her mother was on the happier side of her bi-polar ways but there was no way of knowing until she went inside. She climbed the stairs, and each step seemed to get heavier than the one before. She wondered if there were other people in the world who dreaded coming home to their own house.

Sky reached the top step and then dug into her pocket for the door key. She aimed the key for the lock, but the knob turned and the door snatched open. Startled, Sky looked up.

It was Chance.

He flinched back a bit as if he was startled himself. For a fraction of a second their eyes met and Sky re-lived whatever it was that she felt when they started into each other's eyes when they were in her mother's kitchen.

He cleared his throat.

"Oh... Excuse me. I didn't see you, I mean---"

He was tongue twisted and she giggled at his nervousness. Surprisingly, she had her own set of jitters.

"It's okay." She said.

Chance stepped to the side and put his back against the door.

"Let me just get out of your way."

Sky loved his manners but didn't say anything in response. She stepped through the doorway and eased by him catching the scent of a mild soap as she passed. Sky adored a good smelling man.

Once she cleared his space, she remembered how he had come to her rescue when his friends were being ignorant. She wanted to thank him but decided against it thinking that he might have forgotten about the incident and she continued to walk without giving him another thought.

"Excuse me." He called out. *"Excuse me young lady."*

Sky spun around with a jolt as if him calling out to her was what she was waiting for. She looked into his face and the scar across his cheek caught her attention. She wondered what happened to him. He reached up and touched it as if he was self-conscious about it and she felt guilty for staring at it.

"Yes." She answered politely.

He let his hand fall from his face and he gazed down upon her with thought and began to speak. His lips looked as soft as his eyes.

"I apologize for calling out of your name but I haven't' had the pleasure of getting to know what your name is."

Again she admired his respect and took a few steps toward him with her hand extended.

"My name is Sky... Amber Sky... And you are?"

He took her hand with the firm grip of a man but shook it delicately.

115

"My name is Chance. It's nice to meet you, and by the way, that is a lovely name. Where did it come from, if you don't mind me asking?"

"No I don't mind." Sky couldn't believe that she was engaging one of Dustin's friends. *"My father gave me the name and thank you for the compliment. You have a rather unique name yourself. How did you end up with a name like Chance?"*

His face flushed with embarrassment.

"I don't believe I'm about to tell you this, I've never told anyone. But I'll tell you if you promise to keep it a secret."

She thought his little game was amusing so she went along with it.

"Okay, you have a deal."

He smiled and then took a deep breath.

"Oh God... But anyway look, I got the name Chance because when my mother was pregnant with me, my father told her that he didn't want to be with her any longer and that I was the only chance she had for him to stick around... but a month after I was born, he disappeared never to be seen or heard from again. My mother, not wanting to believe that he was gone, decided to name me Chance with hopes that one day he would return. She always called me her one and only Chance."

A wave of pity swarmed Sky and she felt like she had just invaded his privacy by asking him about his name.

"I'm, I'm, I'm sorry... I didn't mean to be nosy."

"It's cool, you weren't being nosy. And besides, if I never had the name, you would have never asked about it."

He smiled and a weight lifted off of her as he continued to attempt to make her feel better.

"I mean, it wasn't you who left, right?"

"I guess."

They shared a laugh and Chance came out of left field with his next words.

"Anyway, this reason I stopped you is because I was wondering if I could get your phone number so that I could call you sometime."

The question smacked Sky in the face and she was completely thrown off of her pivot. The last thing she expected was to be asked for her phone number by him.

Her eyes ran away from his face in search of safety. She looked around in the air as if the answer to his question could be found there. In an effort to by herself some time, she repeated his words.

"Can you have my phone number?"

She didn't want to flat out say no and be rude about it, but there was no way that she was about to give her number to anyone who willingly associated themselves with Dustin. And not only that, but even if Chance wasn't a friend of Dustin's, Sky still considered herself to be somewhat involved in a relationship with Josh. *'Maybe I should be committed for thinking like this but hey, it is what it is. I am a loyal female and that is how I carry myself.'*

"Umm. Well, I'm sort of involved with someone and I don't think that giving you my number will be appropriate."

Chance's facial expression remained the same as if he wasn't' affected at all by the letdown. But in His eyes, Sky saw the disappointment.

"No problem... No disrespect intended... I apologize if I in any way offended you."

"You didn't offend me. And actually I'm glad you stopped me. I never had the chance to thank you for what you did for me the other day."

His face frowned up in confusion. *"What I did for you?"*

"Yeah; remember the other day when you made our friends move off of the steps so that I could get by?"

"Oh! Yeah, I remember. But you don't have to thank me for thank me for that. It was no big deal."

They stood quiet in a moment of awkwardness. Sky wanted to tell him that it was a really big deal, but she didn't; she wanted to ask him why did he hangout with such people, but she didn't; and she wanted to ask him did her really think she was the most beautiful girl in the world, but she didn't.

Chance looked like he wanted to say something, and he did.

He began to back away and as he did so, he looked at her once again, with eyes full of so much sincerity that they were able to move Sky's heart.

His words were tender.

"Well tell whoever it is that you are involved with that he is the luckiest man in the world."

Then Chance turned around and walked away.

Sky closed the door behind him and wondered if she should have given him her phone number.

AMBER SKY
A.R. DASH

CHAPTER 9.

AMBER SKY
A.R. DASH

Another week crawled by of Sky locking herself inside of her room. She avoided her mother and Dustin at all cost. The only time she left the room was to do the house cleaning when her mother called for her. Other than that, she'd been out of the house one time when she went out to buy herself an outfit and a pair of shoes for Josh's nephew's party. The party was to take place in a couple of days.

Sky was happy, because her mother didn't bother her much. She assumed that her mother's consideration was a band aid to cover the guilt she felt for the things that had been taking place.

Charlene had even tried to make peace a few times by coming into Sky's room and trying to bond with her. But Sky didn't fall for it. She wished that the phony attempt at motherly love was real, but she knew it wasn't. It was just another side effect to her mother's bi-polar ways, and she entertained her mother for no other reason than the fact that her mother was the law of the land.

Charlene hadn't even mentioned anything else about Sky having to move out of her house, but the threat hung over Sky's head like a dark cloud. She would be a fool to forget it.

Sky stood in the middle of her room adoring her new outfit as it lay across her bed. The vanilla cream and pink strapless dress was still in the plastic. She had to look amazing when she finally got to meet Josh's family this coming up weekend.

Josh was on his way to pick her up and he'd told her to dress comfortable because he wanted to go for a walk in the park. Sky was in great spirits because she'd never done such a thing with him before. *'Finally-'* she thought to herself, *'-this is really happening'*.

Sky turned around and looked at herself in the body length mirror. Her five foot four inch frame was cutely dressed in a pair of red denim skin tight jeans. She turned to the side to exam her butt and smiled. The jeans cuffed her behind perfectly. On her feet she had a pair of all white tennis shoes, and up top she had on an all-white cut off t-shirt that left her sexy flat stomach exposed. Her skin was flawless.

Across the shirt, in big ruby red letters was the word *'Sorry'*. And her rusty red hair was pulled back into a tight ponytail that made her honey drop eyes look Asian.

She finished her outfit off by putting on some shiny red strawberry lip gloss. Her phone vibrated and she grabbed it and saw a text from Josh. *'I'm outside'*.

Sky felt the usual flutters in her stomach that she felt when he came around but she shook them off and then blew herself a kiss in the mirror.

"Here I come baby."

She took one last look at the dress lying on the bed and thought about bringing it to show him to see if he liked it but decided against it. She was confident enough to know that he would, so she place it back into her closet and shot out of her room.

She dashed through the house and saw everyone sitting in the living room. Quickly she stopped and gave baby Lilly a kiss and then did the same thing to Autumn.

"Have a good time." Said Charlene.

Sky forced a phony smile and waved a courteous hand in her mother's direction. Then she grabbed the door knob and heard Dustin's voice.

"See you later Amber Sky."

Sky was about to turn around and flip him the finger but instead she darted out of the house and slamming the door behind her.

She walked down the stairs mumbling to herself.

AMBER SKY
A.R. DASH

"Forgive me daddy, but I think I hate that man. You see what's going on. Can you please ask God to soften that man's soul for me?"

Sky sent her prayer up to heaven then jumped into the passenger seat of Josh's car. He kissed her on the lips, turned up the radio and pulled off without giving her one single compliment. Something was wrong with him and she knew it.

They rode in silence and half way through the ride she reached for the radio and turned it down than look at him.

"Are you okay Josh? It seems like you have something on your mind."

His words were curt. *"I'm good."*

He reached for the radio and turned it back up and didn't say anything else until they were on their stroll through the park.

The park was full of life and the midafternoon held a perfect temperature. Children played the way children are supposed to play and a few joggers steadily paced themselves along the path of the park. Everywhere Sky looked, she saw loving couples walking hand and hand, so she reached out and grabbed Josh's hand and interlocked their fingers. His hand was stiff.

A scene of a couple who had a blanket spread out underneath the shade of an oak tree caught Sky's attention. There was a picnic basket was on top of the blanket and the couple sat and talked like they were the only two people in the world. It was breathtaking. Sky looked up and saw a few clouds hiding the sun, and a lonely airplane gliding across the horizon. Then, from somewhere inside of the green trees, she heard beautiful birdsong echo through the park.

This was what Sky imagined when she thought about how mature couples spent their time together. She felt as though she was about to become a part of such a relationship, but that hope quickly faded.

She and Josh walked alongside a lovely small pond only for her to find out that the walk was the beginning of a series of events that would change her life forever.

They walked hand and hand and in unison and he turned to her with something heavy in his eyes.

His voice dragged with sadness.

"I have some bad news."

Sky's initial reaction was one of worry.

"Are you okay Josh? What's the matter?"

He looked away from her and just stared at the ground; like he was intentionally ignoring her. Sky had a quick reflection of when she assumed that he was involved in some kind of illegal activity.

Her heart skipped a beat.

"Josh what's going on? Are you in some kind of trouble?"

"No... No... No... I'm not in any trouble. It's nothing like that, it's just---"

His voice grew distant. He brought his eyes up to Sky's face then looked away quickly as if he couldn't look her in the eyes. She didn't like his awkward actions so she stopped and jerked her hand away from his.

He stopped and turned around to face her.

"Josh, what is wrong? What bad news are you talking about? You are starting to scare me."

AMBER SKY
A.R. DASH

He opened his mouth and sucked in some air. Suddenly he looked like he had come down with a case of the *'I hope she believe me blues'*.

Alarms sounded in Sky's head. Whatever he was about to say was going to be a lie. Then, as if struck by a bolt of lightning, it hit her. Whatever he was about to say had something to do with him taking her to his nephew's birthday party. She knew she'd guessed right, but hearing the words was a devastating blow that she could have never been prepared for.

"We can't go to my nephew's party this weekend---" he paused and looked for Sky's reaction. Sky felt a dark shadow over take her and she stood silent in fury. Josh continued *"I have to work this weekend baby."*

Sky's heart sank to the bottom of her body and her hopes of meeting his family quickly vanished. Next went the feeling of being a part of a normal relationship. Sky tried to hide behind a tight poker face but couldn't. Her eyebrows frowned in disappointing anger.

"No Josh... Please tell me that you are kidding me?"

He continued to stare down at her with insecure eyes. His eyes were a mirror to his soul and from where Sky stood, Josh's soul was full of it.

She took a step back away from him and turned to face the pond. She folded her arms under her breast as the truth of the matter set in. Sky stared blankly at the water with her back to Josh and spoke the words that were on her heart.

"I should've known something like this was going to happen." Slowly she shook her head from side to side. *"Why do I allow you to do this to me? Why do I do this to myself?"*

A terrible storm stirred inside of her. She felt his hand touch her shoulder.

"Sky---"

She spun around with a jolt and looked him directly in his face. He jumped back and she didn't give him a chance to finis another lie.

"Don't touch me! Why are you messing with my head like this? Is it because I'm young? What do you think I am, stupid? You never planned on taking me to that party... Did you?"

He forced his face to appear like he was experiencing some type of discomfort, as if the situation at hand was also hurtful to him. But he didn't say anything. Sky continued to glare at him in wait of an answer. Any other time she would have eased up on Josh when he put on his sympathetic face, but not this time. There was no way that she was about to let him get away with this crime against her heart. His mask of pity meant nothing.

She stepped up into his face. Her arms were still folded beneath her chest and he still hadn't answered her question.

Her voice darkened.

"I'm talking to you Josh. Did you ever really plan on taking me to that party?"

"Come on Sky, what type of question is that? Of course I did. Actually-" His face transformed into a weak smile. *"-All hope is not lost. I'm still trying to see if I can get out of work. I will know by tomorrow... now can we just go and get a room? I've missed you so much baby."*

He reached out to touch her but she jerked away.

"I told you not to touch me! Are you crazy?"

She resisted an urge to slap him in his lying mouth. Her body was on fire. For the first time in almost seven months she accepted the fact that Josh was only using her for her body.

Her voice calmed to a low and hoarse tone.

"All you've ever done was lie to me, and all you've ever wanted from me is sex. What did I ever do to you to deserve this Josh?"

"Deserve what? What am I doing to you? Sky, I love yo---"

"Stop!!! Just Stop!!! Please!!! I can't take it anymore. I just can't!"

He stepped towards her with open arms.

"I know you're upset, but come here baby."

She pushed his arms away from her.

"Don't call me that. I'm not your baby. All I am is a cheap thrill to you."

"Don't say that Sky, you know that's not true."

"It is true Josh! That's why we never go anywhere except for cheap motels. This whole walk through the park was just a scheme to build me up before you tore me down! Maybe you should have waited until after you screwed me to tell me the bad news, because there's not a chance that I'm about to let you touch me now!"

Sky raised her voice.

"What did you think? That you were going to bring me to the park and break my heart and then take me to the motel and sex me until I forgot about your lies?"

"No Sky... I want more than sex from you. I love you and you know it."

'Another lie' she thought. Then she screamed. *"Stop lying to me!"*

Her words carried over to a group of kids playing nearby but she didn't care and she continued to shout.

"Are you ever going to stop with the lies! I don't want to hear them anymore! I refuse to let you take advantage of me any longer!"

Josh stood there like the cat had his tongue. A vision of Sky's mother passed through her mind and she was not about to let Josh do her the way Dustin does her mother.

Josh's expression was neutral. He didn't even look sorry and that bothered Sky more.

"Look at you Josh... You don't even care."

There was no use in keeping herself worked up. She was never one for beating a dead horse so once she realized that her words were going in one ear and out the other, she gave up the battle. She just wanted to be locked in her room.

"Matter of fact, just take me home Josh. I can't be around you right now."

His response was a simple three words. *"Are you sure?"*

Sky's temperature shot up. She squinted her eyes and spoke her next words slowly.

"Take-me-home-Josh."

He didn't try to persuade her any longer. The corner of his mouth curled into an attitude and he turned a cold shoulder to her and walked towards his car. Sky followed behind him like an upset child.

Suddenly drizzles of rain began to fall. Mother Nature must have felt Sky's pain and started to cry for her. Sky looked up and saw nothing but dark clouds. Maybe it was her father crying for her.

Josh didn't look back once to even see if Sky was behind him. Although they were in the middle of a disagreement, him not turning to check on her, somehow still managed to hurt.

The ride was just as disturbing.

She said nothing to him, and he made no attempt to speak to or comfort her. He drove in silence and kept whatever thoughts he was having to himself.

Josh pulled the vehicle into a gas station. He looked to the convenient store and then he looked at Sky like he was about to ask her if she wanted something, but he didn't. He just hopped out of the car with an attitude and walked through the falling sun shower as if the rain didn't bother him.

Sky laughed to herself. *"He acts like he has a reason to be upset... pssst."*

Sky reached up for the sun visor to see if she looked as stupid as she was feeling. She pulled the visor down and the plastic envelope fell into her lap for a second time. She picked it up. The front of it had a clear plastic casing and through it, she saw that she was holding the vehicles registration and insurance card. She ignored it and looked up into the mirror.

Just as she expected, she saw a fool staring back at her. She could barely look herself in the face so she looked away and was about to stuff the documents back into the cuff of the visor, but she caught a glimpse of something that she thought was strange.

The name on the registration did not say Josh. The vehicle was registered to someone name *Calvin B. Jones.* Suspicion ran through Sky's body. She wondered if Josh's name wasn't Josh. What if his name was really *Calvin B. Jones.* A touch of fear knotted Sky's stomach. She looked towards Josh and saw him chuckling with the cute cashier. Then she turned her attention back to the documents.

The vehicle's insurance card was wedged behind the registration and she slid it out. It had the same name typed across it. *Calvin B. Jones.* She continued to study the insurance card and what she saw next caused the hairs on the back of her neck to stand up. Whomever *Calvin B. Jones* was, lived at 200 Kennedy Boulevard. And Kennedy Boulevard was only a few streets away from where Sky lived. Sky didn't know what to think or do.

She looked at Josh again and saw the cashier handing him his change. The cashier had a bashful smile on her face and Sky wondered what was so funny. Quickly she pushed the concern from her mind. There was no time to be worrying about his flirtatious ways…

Josh began to back away from the counter without taking his eyes off of the cashier. With the swiftness of a magician and the fear of the unknown stalking her, Sky stuffed the documents back into the envelope. Mistakenly, she placed the insurance card at the front and not the registration card. She hoped he wouldn't notice.

She kept her eyes on him as he said whatever last words to the cashier, and just before he looked towards the vehicle, Sky jammed the documents up into the visor and slammed it shut.

Josh looked away from the cashier and directly at Sky. His smile turned into a frown.

"You no good--- Umm." Sky mumbled.

Josh stepped outside of the store and jogged towards the car. The closer he got, the more unease she felt. He jumped into the driver's seat and pulled off without saying a word to her and Sky was happy that they weren't speaking. It made it that much easier to hide her fear.

Josh slowed the car down as it approached Sky's mother house and she had never been happier to see the house of horrors.

AMBER SKY
A.R. DASH

The vehicle hadn't come to a complete stop before Sky had the door open. As soon as it did stop, she jumped out without as much as looking at him.

"Sky!" he called out.

She froze with one foot hanging out of the door and her back still to him. She didn't want to turn around out of fear that he would be able to detect something being wrong from the look on her face.

She spoke with her back to him. *"What Josh?"*

"You can't even give me enough respect to turn around and look at me while we talk?"

"Respect-" Sky kept the rest of her ugly thoughts to herself. *"What do you want Josh?"*

"I promise to make this up to you the next time my family has a gathering, okay?"

Sky wanted to scream and to let him know where he could shove him and his family's next gathering, but instead, she stepped completely out of the car and held the door open and then bent down to look at him. Light drizzles of rain fell on her.

"You be sure to do that Josh, okay... I'll be waiting."

She slammed the door and turned around and walked towards the house. Over her shoulder she heard the car pull off and she stopped walking and couldn't help but to look at it until it was out of her sight. Then she shot up the stairs into the house and locked the door behind her like she was just being chased.

Once she was inside she caged herself up in her room and got undressed and laid across her bed and tried to dissect everything she knew about the man name Josh; which wasn't much. The only hardcore information she had was 200 Kennedy Boulevard.

After an hour of debating with herself on what she should do, she made a decision to find out the truth. She put her clothes back on and left her house on a mission to find 200 Kennedy Boulevard.

CHAPTER 10.

AMBER SKY
A.R. DASH

Kennedy Boulevard is one of those streets that ran the entire distance of the city. It was also only about six city blocks away from where Sky lived.

The sun shower had passed over and the day was just starting to dawn. Sky wore a thin Jacket over her ripped t-shirt because the sun shower had left a light chill. The ground was still wet from the rain and Sky took uncertain steps as she approached the intersection of Kennedy Boulevard and Third Avenue. She looked both ways at the distance of Kennedy and thought of how it ran from one end of the city to the other.

'I don't even know which way to go'. She told herself. But the truth was that she needed a reason to not go through with what she was about to do. And not wanting to walk through the whole city was about a good enough reason as any. She stood on the corner pondering what she should do next.

Traffic was light; an occasional car passed by her and one time a man who looked to be in his fifties slowed his car and showed her some interest. He stopped the car directly in front of her and rolled the window down.

"Hey sweetie? What's your name?"

He was old enough to be her father and she felt disgusted.

"I'm only fifteen." She said.

And she started walking. But he didn't care. He pulled the car alongside her.

"Get in sweetie. Let me give you a ride."

Sky pulled out her phone and flashed it in his direction.

"Get lost or I'm going to call the cops."

The car sped away without further incident.

"What am I doing out her?" she asked herself.

AMBER SKY
A.R. DASH

She was about to turn around and call the whole investigation off but something made her look up at the first house on the corner. The number *82* was in big silver numbers on the door. That meant that *200* Kennedy Boulevard was closer than she imagined. But it was in the other direction. Sky took a deep breath and turned around. *'This is something that I have to do.'*

She started walking and suddenly she thought about calling Danielle for some advice. But Danielle would probably try to talk her out of it and tell her to just leave Josh alone. But Sky couldn't; she had to find out if his name was really *Calvin B. Jones.* And if it was, Sky was going to drag him out of *200* Kennedy Boulevard by his ears and make him do some serious explaining.

Sky walked casually and surveyed the neighborhood. The sidewalks were clean, the lawns were well kept, and there was a nice model car parked in each driveway. Sky analyzed the area to belong to middle class working families. She couldn't help but to play close attention to every house and car that she passed, because not one of the houses or cars would she mind owning for herself. Then a vision of Josh jumped into her mind. She could definitely picture him living in the type of neighborhood she was walking through.

Sky wondered if in fact this was Josh's neighborhood; *'not even ten blocks away from where I live'*. A cold chill touched her and she wrapped her arms around her body and crossed the intersection of Kennedy Boulevard and Fourth Avenue.

Sky looked at the first house on the corner. The numbers on the door read *128*. *'not much further'* she thought to herself. *'What if he does live in this neighborhood? What if all of these houses I'm looking at belong to his neighbors?'* Sky's mind continued to race as if her conscious was trying to tell her something.

She reached the corner of Fifth Avenue and Kennedy Boulevard and the house on the corner said *160*.

She realized that she wasn't too far away from the mystery address and the same fear that she felt when she was looking at the registration card took hold of her. Wild butterflies swarmed her stomach. She slowed her pace but willed herself to keep moving forward.

The area was mostly quiet except for a pair of teen boys playing basketball on a roll-away-hoop in a driveway. A crime watch sign caught Sky's attention and the thought of Josh being involved in some kind of illegal activity crossed her mind again.

170

Sky walked by 170 Kennedy Boulevard and the wild butterflies in her stomach were replaced by tight knots.

180

She reached 180 Kennedy Boulevard and decided to cross to the other side of the street. She had no reason for doing it.

190

'What did you do to me Josh?'

200.

From the other side of the street, Sky looked up and saw *200* Kennedy Boulevard. Josh's car was parked in the driveway of the house. She no longer had any doubt. This was definitely his address.

She studied the house carefully. It was a typical blue old Victorian two-family home that appeared to be well taken care of. A curiosity grew inside of her. *'What does it look like on the inside?'*

Her eyes landed back on the car that she'd just been a passenger in not even two hours ago. She stood across the street from the house not knowing what she should do next.

She stayed on the other side of the street behind a car mentally torturing herself.

'Think...Think...Think...'

She thought harder.

"Think Sky, think."

She knew that she couldn't stand there just string at the house. Someone might see her and her presence could raise some suspicion. The neighborhood was so calm that someone may even call the police if they saw her just standing there. She had to do something, but what?

She watched the house for movement but didn't see any. But she knew for a fact that Josh was in the house because not a full two hours had passed since they were together.

"Are what the heck, it's either now or never."

Sky stepped into the street and walked towards the house. Her plan was simple. She was going to march up the stairs and ring the doorbell and then ask for Josh by name. *'What was the worst that could happen? After all, he is my man and I have been sleeping with him for more than half of a year'.*

Before she walked up the steps she just so happen to look into his car and saw a baby seat. *"A baby chair!"* she said out loud. *"Where the hell did that come from?"* she looked up at the house. *"Something's not right."*

There were six steps to climb and she took them one at a time. As soon as she stepped onto the porch, her heart pounded at the sight of a mini blue and white tricycle. Her mind flashed back to the pacifier that was wedged between the seat. Whoever the baby was, definitely lived at the address as well. Sky's heart rate increased because the situation was becoming all too real. *'I should just ask Josh to tell me the truth'.* She thought. *'I can't go through with this'.* Sky spun around and was about to shoot back down the stairs but the sound of the door unlocking caused her to freeze with fear.

Her feet got as heavy as cinder blocks. The door slowly creaked open and slowly she turned around.

Josh came into view holding a little baby boy in his arms. The baby looked about three and he was sucking on the blue pacifier.

Josh's face fell to the floor. They both stood there stuck with blank looks on their faces.

Josh sounded like he was looking at his worst enemy and he spoke just above a whisper.

"What are you doing here?"

Sky didn't have a chance to say anything. Over Josh's shoulder a voice called out.

"Who are you talking to Calvin? Who is that at the door?"

Sky and Josh stared at each other like they both knew they were in trouble. Neither one of them was able to speak. Josh's face turned pale and the female who had called him Calvin came stepping from behind him into the doorway. It was Danielle.

Blood rushed to Sky's head and she felt herself get dizzy.

Danielle's face looked just as stunned as everyone else's.

"Sky what are you doing here? How did you know where I lived?"

Danielle asked the question as if she thought Sky was there to see her. Sky was unable to move or speak. All she could do was blink. When Danielle didn't get a response, she looked at Josh and saw that he had the same dumbfounded look as Sky. And it didn't take long for her to put the puzzle together.

She looked from Josh back to Sky and back to Josh then back to Sky.

"What is going on right now?... Do you two know each other or something?"

They looked at each other, but neither one of them said a word.

Danielle's voice hardened. *"One of you needs to say something and say it now."* She looked into her husband's face. *"Calvin!"* she screamed.

He still didn't say anything, but Sky did.

"Danielle... this is my boyfriend Josh."

Danielle took a step back and looked at Sky like she was crazy.

"What?"

Sky saw danger in Danielle's face so she swallowed hard and her heart hammered in her chest.

"This is Josh that I was telling you about."

Danielle lost it.

"His name aint no damn Josh! This is my husband Calvin! What are you talking about Sky? Are you telling me that you have been sleeping with my husband?"

Danielle lunged at Sky in a fit of rage. *"You whore!!!"*

Sky didn't have time to react. Danielle shoved her backwards and Sky felt the wind woosh out of her chestand she fell over the tricycle. Her body crashed onto the porch. Sky's instinct told her that she was in trouble but Danielle was too quick. She dived on top of Sky and swung her fist as fast and hard as she could.

"Smack!"

"Smack!"

"Smack!"

"How could you! He is my husband!!!"

"Smack!"

"Smack!"

"Smack!"

Then Sky felt Danielle's hand tightening around her throat and everything started to get black.

Sky couldn't breathe and she didn't know what was happening but the attack suddenly stopped. Danielle was no longer on top of her. She blinked her eye's to focus and saw that Josh had Danielle in a tight bear hug with her legs kicking wildly. She wanted to get loose. She wanted more of Sky.

Sky jumped to her feet. Her face was wet and the taste of warm blood leaked into her mouth. She looked around frantically and then took off running. From behind, she heard Danielle screaming.

"I'm gonna kill you."

Sky looked back and saw that Danielle had gotten free from Josh and was coming behind her, but Sky had too much of a head start to be caught. Sky ran with all of her strength and never looked back at 200 Kennedy Boulevard again.

CHAPTER 11.

Sky screamed. *"Just leave me alone!!!"* Her voice echoed off of her bedroom walls. *"Just-leave-me-alone!!! You are sick!!!"*

She mashed the end call button on her cellphone before Josh had a chance to speak. Then she dropped down onto her bed and squeezed her cellphone in her hand to stop herself from slamming it on the floor.

She thought about the man named Calvin and let out a pinned up grunt.

"Ughh!!!"

Her bedroom door was closed but she still could hear her mother and Dustin arguing. She pointed her head towards the ceiling.

"Whyyyy!!!"

Sky felt a migraine coming on so she put her phone down on the bed and reached up for her butterfly pendant, but it wasn't there. Somehow during the attack from Danielle, it was popped from her neck and lost.

Sky dropped her face down into both of her hands and took a deep breath to try to calm her nerves. It had been a week since she'd found out the truth about Josh and ever since that day she'd been locked up in her room trying to figure out how she'd gotten herself mixed up in such a bizarre situation.

Although it was true, she did not want to believe that Josh's name was really Calvin B. Jones; or for that matter, C.J., Danielle's Husband. Sky replayed the series of events a thousand times in her head and she could find no justifications for the fact that she had been sleeping with Danielle's husband.

The next day after Danielle had attacked her, Sky's phone rang and she looked down and saw Danielle's number. Sky thought that Danielle was calling to talk the disaster over, but that wasn't the case.

Sky accepted the call with a fragile voice.

"Hello?"

Danielle was crying.

"You're wrong Sky! Youre wrong! You were sleeping with my husband and you ruined my marriage and my family. I hate you Sky! I hate you!"

"But-but-but Danielle, I didn't know---"

"Shut up!!! Shut up!!! I hate you !!! and I swear that this is not over Sky."

Click...

Now, a week later, Sky was still as confused as ever.

She picked her head up out of her hands and looked at her phone. *'Why was I such a fool?'*

She looked back on her relationship with Josh and realized that she always knew that something wasn't right about him and she only had herself to blame for ignoring the signs that flashed like bright lights in her face; him only coming around on weekends; him telling her that he couldn't carry a phone because of his work; them only going to motels and never out in public... the list went on and on.

Sky took the blame for everything because just like her father always said *'when people do you wrong, they're not one hundred percent at fault. You hold some of the blame for allowing them to do you wrong'*.

Sky continued to stare at the phone then she spoke out loud. *"He wasn't even considerate enough to tell me his real name; never mind the fact that he was married with children"*

Sky now had the experience of being the mistress of a cheating husband.

She picked up her phone and thought about Danielle. Her hand found its way up to the left side of her face and she gently touched the small cut she suffered at the hands of ex-only friend.

Sky wasn't mad at Danielle's reaction. What she was mad at was losing Danielle's friendship. If she could, she would make everything right, but she was certain that there was no way to fix what she had broken.

Sky would be forced to let Danielle go. Along with losing the friendship, she also had to let go or her hopes of becoming a mail lady because Danielle made it her business to have someone personally call Sky to let her know that she wasn't being considered for the job. Her dreams of having her own place with her siblings had once again been killed.

Sky was crushed to the point of devastation and she'd been crying all week but she refused to cry anymore. She just had to do everything on her own like she always did and that was all there was to it.

When her thoughts came back from wherever they were, Sky heard her mother and Dustin still arguing. For the entire week that Sky had been caged up in the room, it seemed as the two of them argued more and more. The sounds of their voices irked her almost to the point of insanity. She was at a breaking point and just wanted to explode. Their voices went back and forth.

Sky Screamed.

"Just shut up already!"

She didn't even care if they heard her.

Her room door burst open and her neck snapped up to see who it was. It was Autumn. Her sporadic reaction made Autumn stop short.

"It's only me Sky."

The sight of her younger sister literally warmed her body.

"Hey lil sis. What's up?"

Autumn stepped into the room.

"Nothing, I just heard you screaming so I came to see if you were okay."

Sky felt loved.

"Awww. Thank you. I'm okay. Just tired of them two arguing."

"Me too." Said Autumn. Then she went and sat next to Sky.

The door was now open and Dustin's voice echoed through the house.

"You heard me woman! I'm not driving to no hospital and sitting in no waiting room for five hours just to hear some stupid doctor say that all she has is a little stomach ache! I'm not doing it!"

The more he spoke, the angrier Sky became, and he continued to yell at Charlene.

"Why don't you just give her a laxative or something?"

"Because she is my daughter! And I want to take her to the emergency room. She could be coming down with the flu or something worse."

Sky jumped up and charged towards the door and slammed it.

145

"I can't stand being inside of this house! I swear I can't wait to get out of this place!"

Sky exhaled and then her phone rang. She already knew that it was Josh or Danielle. Her brain thumped and it felt like the walls were closing in on her. The phone rang again. Dustin continue to yell. Sky put her hands over her ears and closed her eyes.

"Why Lord! Why!"

She was so caught up in her own feelings that she forgot about Autumn.

The phone stopped ringing and Sky took her hands from over her ears. She turned around and saw that Autumn had tears in her innocent eyes. Sky rushed over to her sister and sat down on the bed next to her then threw her arms around her.

"I'm sorry autumn... It's just so much going on."

She held Autumn against her chest and noticed that her sister had a fever. Suddenly she recalled her mother and Dustin's argument. For some reason Sky thought that they were talking about baby Lilly but it was Autumn they were talking about taking to the emergency room.

She pulled back away from Autumn and placed the back of her hand on Autumn's forehead. It was warm. She looked at her younger sister inquisitively. Tear tracks were on the child's face.

"Autumn, what's wrong? Are you feeling okay?"

Autumn let out a childish pout and pounded her fist against her leg then whimpered.

"I'm tired of everybody always yelling at each other!"

She looked up into her older sister's face with eyes full of watery questions. Her cries were a true plea for her sister's help.

"I know I was only seven when daddy died, but when he was around, everything was different. It wasn't nothing like this. Everybody was happy when daddy was here. Everybody wasn't always so mad and so mean."

She looked deep into Sky's eyes.

"Sky, I want daddy to come back."

Then she bent her head back into Sky's chest, threw her arms around her and bawled like a baby. Sky's heart burst into a million pieces. She didn't know what to say so she just held her sister lovingly. With everything that was going on around in Sky's world, she never took the time to realize how Autumn was being affected.

She wrapped her arms around Autumn and kissed the top of her head.

"It's going to be okay Autumn. I promise... I'm going to make everything right."

She caressed her younger sister's back.

She was about to say that things would be alright as soon as she gets a job, but the words got stuck in her throat. She didn't know where her job was going to come from. Autumn continued to sniffle against her chest and the warm tears soaked through Sky's shirt. All Sky could do was squeeze her tighter.

Sky had no way of explain to Autumn why Dustin was always yelling at their mother and treating her badly; there was no way to explain to her why their mother allowed him to do so; there was now for Sky to explain why she was always locked in her room and barely spoke to anyone in the house.

No… Sky had no answers at all, and the last thing she wanted to do was lie to Autumn at a time when she really needed her.

From somewhere deep in Sky's mind a thought popped into her head of what she might have to do. She remembered the conversation that Dustin and his friends had in front of her house about how to get welfare.

Sky swallowed a big lump of pride then she lifted Autumn up out of her chest and wiped away as many tears as she could.

Then she looked her sister directly in the face.

"Autumn, I'm going to get us out of this house as soon as I can but I need your help. Do you think you can help me?"

Autumn wiped her face and nodded at the same time.

Sky spoke seriously.

"I'm going to do whatever I have to do to get us somewhere else to live but I need you to be strong and to not let the things that's going on around here get to you. Whenever things start to bother you, I want you to remember that it won't be long before we don't have to deal with Dustin no more. Can you do that for me?"

Autumn nodded her head again.

"Good" said sky. Then she put the back of her palm on Autumn's head. *"Now what's wrong with you? It feels like you've come down with a fever."*

"I just don't feel good. For the last couple of days my stomach has been hurting and now I have a fever. I threw up a little while ago and I told mommy and that's when they started arguing. He don't want to drive to the hospital."

Sky didn't bother to get mad. She recalled her nursing school days and from Autumn's symptoms it sounded like she

148

had either come down with food poisoning or maybe a summer cold. But food poisoning seemed more the case.

"It sounds like you have food poisoning, but I don't want you to start worrying because it's not that serious."

Sky poked her finger into Autumn's stomach and made her laugh.

"You're just a big baby."

Autumn giggled. *"Stop poking me."*

Sky got up and walked over to the closet.

"Let me find something to put on and I will ask mommy for some money so that we could get on the bus and go to the hospital."

Autumn's eyes lit up. Her sorrow was disappeared. She acted like Sky had just offered to take her to Disney world.

"Are you serious! Are you really going to take me?"

"Yes."

"Good, I'd rather go with you anyway."

Autumn made the trip sound like so much fun. Sky opened her closet and saw the dress that she was supposed to wear to meet Josh's so called family, and for a second she lost her train of thought. The dress was so pretty, but it just hung in the closet and she would probably never have a reason to wear. *'Maybe I should take it back'.*

Sky's concentration broke when her mother came charging in the room.

Charlene looked at Autumn with frustration.

"Go and get dressed so that I can take you to the hospital to see what's wrong with you."

Autumn tried to protest. *"But--- but, Sky is going---"*

Charlene pointed a threatening finger at her middle daughter.

"Girl! I didn't ask you nothing about Sky...Now go and do what I told you to do... Now!"

Autumn hung her head and mumbled underneath her breath and then she stormed out of the room.

Charlene turned to Sky.

"I need you to keep an eye on Lilly until I get back from the hospital. I don't want her in that waiting room around all of those germs."

It sounded like more of an order then it did a request, and Sky thought to herself, *'if you don't want her around germs you need to get rid of her father'.*

"Why can't Dustin watch her? He's her father."

"Why? Because I don't feel like driving! That's why. Now do you have any more questions?"

She glared at Sky waiting for a challenge. Sky just sucked her teeth and shook her head. Once again her mother had made up an excuse to get Dustin out of his fatherly duties. Sky turned her back to her mother and walked over to her dresser and opened a draw and acted like she was looking for something.

Charlene spoke as if she didn't care for Sky's attitude.

"You want me to bring Lilly in here, or are you coming out there to get her?"

"Just leave her there... I'll be out there to get her in a minute."

Charlene didn't say anything else. She left the room leaving behind a child on fire. Sky balled up her fist and felt a body full of tension. She turned around and looked at the empty doorway. Autumn came walking by with a frown on her face and Sky felt sad for her sister but there was nothing she could do.

Sky didn't leave out of the room until she was sure that her mother was gone.

When she was about to walk out of the room, her cellphone rang and she picked it up and saw a blocked number. she had a good idea of who it was so she hit the end call button and threw the phone on the bed. There was no time to be worrying about what happened with Danielle. Sky had a new problem. She had to figure out how she was going to go about applying for welfare.

CHAPTER
12.

AMBER SKY
A.R. DASH

Half an hour after everyone was cleared out of the house, Sky decided to take Lilly out front to sit on the porch so that they could get some fresh air.

It was about one o'clock on a beautiful summer afternoon. There was just enough clouds in the sky to block the sun from giving off direct rays of blazing heat. A couple of houses over, Sky saw a man about fifty years old handling a lawn mower dominantly and the smell of freshly cut grass lingered in the air. Every so often, a car drove through the bloc, but other than that, the street didn't have much activity.

Sky sat on the porch in a fold away lawn chair with a pair of sunglasses cocked up on her forehead. She looked down at Lilly's baby chair and saw her youngest sister falling asleep. Lilly's head nodded to one side and her pacifier threatened to fall from her mouth. The pacifier dropped from her mouth and Lilly smiled. Sky couldn't help but to smile along with her. She was always told that when a baby smiled in their sleep, it meant that they were playing with the angels.

Sky reached down and pinched the infants smiling cheek lightly.

"Some company you are."

Lilly smiled harder as if she could understand the remark made about her.

For no reason at all, Sky eyes returned to the old man and she watched as he pushed the red machine from one end of his yard to the other. She admired how the neighbor hadn't let his age get in the way of his manliness. It was a characteristic that she could see her father possessing if he were still alive.

Sky twisted her body to both sides, pulled her shades down over her eyes, then sat back in her chair and let herself drift off into her thoughts. Her mind began to haunt her with the ugliness of her reality.

Her first recollection was of the person she'd come to know as Josh. She was beyond happy to have rid herself of such a person, but truth be told, she didn't want to be alone and Josh was gone for good. It wasn't like all of the other times when Josh stayed away for weeks on end at his supposed job. Back then, what kept Sky going was the fact that she knew he would return soon to come and pick her up and take her away from her problems for a while. But those days were long gone and Sky was left to deal with her problems on her own.

The only thoughts that made her feel better when it came to Josh, was knowing that everything could have turned out worse. Josh could have been a serial killer for real, and he could have left her body buried alive somewhere. The thought sent a cold shiver down her spine. *'Daddy told me not to talk to strangers'.* She thought to herself.

Next she thought about Danielle.

Losing Danielle hurt the most. From the moment that they were reunited, Danielle had done nothing but try to help her.

'And how do I repay you? By sleeping with your husband'.

Sky just wished that Danielle understood that she would have never done this to her intentionally. There wasn't a disloyal bone in Sky's body. But there was no way for Danielle to know that.

Then she thought about her current situation and how she now had to go up to welfare to get some public assistance so that she could move her siblings to a better environment. She thought about collecting food stamps and everything that come along with them.

'I am not a welfare case'. She thought.

Then she thought about the tears in Autumn's eyes and remember the promise she made to her.

"I just have to do what I have to do." She said out loud.

Then a vision of her father jumped into her mind and she reached for her butterfly pendant forgetting it was gone. Her words were but a whisper.

"I know you must be turning in your grave Daddy. But I promise you that I will make everything right. I just need a little time."

Lilly slept peacefully. The neighbor mowed ambitiously and Sky spoke seriously to her father's spirit.

"Daddy, I realize the part I've played in this big mess and I take full responsibility. I was beyond naive. Matter of fact, I wasn't naïve, I was flat out stupid. I have been acting like a complete fool and I know you taught me better than that. All of the signs were there when it came to Josh but I chose to ignore them. For some reason I wanted to see past the bad in him, but all I did was put myself in harm's way-"

The burn of awaiting tears stung the wells of her eyes.

"-I didn't want to see the bad in him because I didn't want to be alone. But it's hard down here Daddy. It's hard when you don't have nobody in your corner rooting for you. I thought that things would get better with him so I gave him a chance... But it won't happen again Daddy, I promise. Next time I will be more aware. Matter of fact daddy-"

It was as if she could feel her father's presence there with her.

"-There won't be a next time. I'd rather be alone than to be stupid. You've taught me so much better than that. So I will not give no one else a chance to do to me what I allowed Josh to do. You have my word; so if I don't feel as though the next man to enter into my life was sent by you, then I won't even give him a chance to know my name. You have always known what was best for me and I'm sure that you still do... I will just wait patiently until you send that special someone to me-"

Sky's eyes were squeezed tightly shut beneath the shades because she truly wanted her father to believe what she was saying.

"-Okay daddy? The only way that someone will get a chance at my heart is if you send them to me---"

"Excuse me. Amber Sky..."

Sky's thoughts were interrupted by the sound of someone calling her by her whole name. She opened her eyes and saw Chance standing at the bottom of the steps. For no apparent reason the sight of Dustin's friend bothered her. Maybe she was just mad at all men.

He couldn't see behind the sunglasses but Sky's eyes screamed *'What do you want!'*

"What?" she said stiffly.

It was evident that he knew she didn't want to be bothered by the way he stumbled over his words.

"Excuse me... Uh... umm... I'm umm, sorry to disturb you... but do you know where... I mean."

He couldn't complete a sentence and to Sky he sounded like a complete fool. She continued to stare at him coldly.

Chance looked around nervously like he was looking for something that wasn't there.

Sky couldn't have been more annoyed. She lifted her shades to her forehead.

"Can I help you?"

In that instance, as if Chance had somehow shaken off his nervousness, he seemed to get his feet beneath him. Sky's sharp tone must not have sat well with him. He spoke direct but he was still respectful.

He stood up straight, looked her square in the face and said what he had to say.

"Well I was trying to apologize for disturbing you, but anyway, can you tell me if Dustin is home?"

She didn't answer right away. Instead she sat there for a second holding his gaze. On the inside she was captivated by the look in his eyes, but she didn't show it.

She kept her face stern as she studied him. She noticed that he didn't have the same look he had in his eyes when he was standing in the doorway of the kitchen. This new look was demanding. His eyes were still soft, but he held a touch of hardness; they were just as friendly, but at the same time, more assertive. And the scar underneath his left eye added an edge of mysterious danger to him that Sky liked.

But she didn't let any of these feelings show.

Her response was short.

"No... he's not here."

Chance pushed on.

"Do you know where he is? Or when he will be returning?"

Sky barked.

"Do I look like his keeper? Do I have a leash on him? Do-I-even-look like I care where he is at or when he will be returning?"

Immediately the confidence left Chance's face and was replaced with humility. He had no idea that he was just in the wrong place at the wrong time; he was in the line of fire of a bunch of bullets that weren't meant for him.

He sucked in his lips then nodded his head and spoke gracefully.

"Hey, like I said, I'm sorry to have bothered you. But if you could just tell--- better yet--- never mind. I will tell him myself when I see him."

He backed away from the stairs.

"You just be sure to enjoy the rest of your day."

Chance turned and walked away. Sky stared at his back. Seeing his humble retreat caused her to realize that she may have been disrespectful to him for no reason. Then she remembered how he had come to her rescue when his friends were being idiots.

Chance never looked back, and as he walked, something inside of her started screaming at her and telling her how wrong she was for how she'd conducted herself. Then something else inside of her told her that the rest of the world was cold hearted, so why shouldn't she be.

Then she disliked herself for knowing his name.

She jumped up out of her seat.

"Chance! Hey Chance! Excuse me!!!"

He stopped with a jolt and turned around to face her. She waved her hand in a gesture for him to come back. Lilly had half awaken and started to whine. Sky reached down and placed the pacifier into Lilly's mouth.

Chance returned to the foot of the steps and looked up at Sky with caution. She looked down at him with guilt. She knew she was wrong so there was no need for her to beat around the bush with her apology. *"Hey listen, I called you back because I wanted to apologize for being rude to you a minute ago. You didn't deserve that. Please accept my apology."*

Chance smiled.

"Why thank you. But you didn't have to apologize. We all have our bad days, and besides, I'm quite sure that your anger wasn't really directed towards me."

His response made her realize just how wrong she was. He didn't have to say anything else but he did.

"To be honest Amber Sky, I don't blame you for being the way you are. If I were you, I would be weary of all of Dustin's friends as well. Especially after how I saw them treat you that day on these steps."

His words were sincere, and surprisingly, she didn't mind him calling her by both of her names. She looked down the stairs into his face and felt like she had to explain herself.

"Thank you for being so understanding, I mean, I'm really not a mean person but as of lately, things have been kind of crazy for me."

He smiled.

"No problem, and I appreciate the apology."

Neither one of them said anything else and then Chance turned to walk away.

Sky spoke to his back without thinking.

"Why do they act like that?"

Chance stopped walking and turned to her with an inquisitive look on his face.

"Excuse me?"

"Your friends-" she said. *"-why don't they have any respect?"*

Unexpectedly, Chance let out a little chuckle. Then he moved back into the direction of the steps. Carefully he looked up at her.

"To be honest with you, I have no clue why they act the way they do. But you can't put all of the blame on them-"

Sky's forehead wrinkled before he could finish his sentence.

"-You have to blame the circus for letting them clowns run loose."

Sky burst out in a much needed laughter. *'He has a sense of humor'.* She thought... and while giggling she studied his face.

Chance wasn't a bad looking man. He had neat shoulder length dreadlocks; his skin was the color of a penny, and he had nice square jaws; his eyes were a little wider than slants and the scar that ran across his cheek to his ear added just the right amount of roughness to make him look like the kind of guy you didn't want to test.

Sky felt an urge to keep the conversation going.

"Well I have another question if you don't mind me asking?"

"No I don't mind at all. Ask away."

"I don't mean to be judgmental, but you don't seem, to fit into their little crowd; so why do you choose them as your friends?"

He raised a finger into the air.

"Hold on for a second. I don't mean to change the subject, but was that a compliment you just gave? If so, I am honored, but did you really just compliment one of Dustin's friends?"

160

The corners of his mouth curled into a flirtatious smile.

Sky responded with a smile of her own.

"You know what? I can't believe what I am about to say, but yes I did give a compliment to a friend of Dustin's... I think you deserve it."

She meant every word that she spoke. She really felt as though he was extremely different from the people he hung out with. And speaking to him only made her more eager to know the answer to her question.

"So why do you hang out with those guys?"

Chance inhaled, and then he folded in his lips. Then he hung his head and shook it from side to side as if he was in some way ashamed.

When he looked back up at Sky, he was still smiling, but Sky could tell that it was a mask.

"You know something Amber Sky-"

He paused as if to take thought. Sky liked to hear him call her by both of her names.

"-I really don't know why I hang out with them. But if I had to be honest with you, I would tell you that I wasn't always so different from them."

"I'm sorry but that's a little hard to believe... You just don't seem like the type who goes around disrespecting females at every chance you get."

The smile faded and there was nothing left but shame. Sky could see that he was touch by the topic.

"Again Amber Sky, I have to be honest... In the past, yes I have been just as ignorant as they are...and sometimes even worse."

Suddenly, Sky's mind was invaded by a thought of Chance attacking her the way that Dustin had, and a thought of discomfort settled in her stomach. Her mind was bothered and she wondered why the thought meant anything to her. After all, he did confess out of his own mouth that he was no different from the rest of them.

Sky somehow found a way to move on in her thought process but instead of speaking to him, the sarcasm in her tone made it sound as if she was speaking at him.

Harmlessly he stood at the foot of the steps.

"So Chance, what made you change? Did some girl get tired of your disrespect and fight you back? Because I know if my father hadn't raised me the way he did---"

Her mind drifted to when Dustin had her pinned against the counter. If she could have reached that knife she probably would've used it.

"---put it like this. If I wasn't a lady, some of you would really be in trouble."

She was so caught in the moment that she didn't even realize that she'd included him in her threat.

"---or did the girl that you loved break you little heart? And now you realize that you should have done things differently."

She didn't give him a chance to respond and his long face was proof that she was hitting nerve after nerve.

Unconsciously, she wanted her words to hurt him. She hoped that he was re-living whatever aha moment it was that made him turn away from her disrespectful ways. She wanted him to feel as bad as she wished Josh felt for doing to her what he did.

Chance stood lost in a sad moment, but Sky had no sympathy for him. He deserved whatever torment he was feeling.

Sky thought again about what she would've done if she had grabbed the knife when Dustin attacked her and she decided to throw salt on Chance's wounds.

"---or did someone get tired of your mess and cut you across your face."

Chance turned his head like he could no longer look her in the face. He stared blankly at the lawn mower man who'd finally finished mowing his yard. Slowly Chance looked back up the stairs. Lilly still slept quietly and Sky stood there almost heartless. Intently his eyes took hold of her.

His face forced a stiff smile that did little to hide his hurt.

"Let's just put it like this Sky... I did a lot of foolish things, and I did lose someone I loved---"

"It didn't feel good to you, did it?"

"No I can't say that it did."

"So who did your foolishness cost you? Your little girlfriend?" she wouldn't let up. *"What happened? Or are you to ashamed to talk about it?"*

Sky lashed out her frustrations on Chance and as she did so she felt a strange sense of empowerment. For the first time in her life, she wasn't the one on the receiving end of the abuse, and oddly, it felt good. If she had been this way with Dustin and Josh and everyone else that she came in contact with, then maybe they wouldn't have taken so much advantage of her. Sky decided that from this moment forward, she would be this cold with everybody. Maybe even her mother.

Chance stared at the bottom step and then up at Sky.

"If you must know, no I didn't lose a girlfriend. But I'll tell you what; since I know you can see that this topic is sorely affecting me; and just for the sake of whatever's making you enjoy this, I will tell you what made me change, and who I lost-"

Sky remained stone faced.

"-but before I tell you anything, I just want you to know that whatever Dustin and the rest of those guys do to you is no different from what you're doing to me right now."

The feeling of Dustin having her bent back over the kitchen sink with his hands jammed in her pants jumped into her mind. There was nothing in life that Sky was capable of doing that could compare to that.

Chance's accusation caused her temperature to climb. Dustin tried to take the most precious thing that she possessed, and she couldn't believe that Chance had the audacity to say that she was the same as that animal.

She really didn't want to hear any more of his words. She was drugged with the feeling of being a cold blooded predator and not the sheepish prey that she always was. Sky's life was bottled up inside of her, and finally she had an opportunity to let some of her frustrations out.

Her words were razor sharp.

"First of all, there are a whole lot of things that make me different from people like you and Dustin. You know that just as well as I do... And secondly, all I did was ask you a simple question. I didn't---"

Chance held an open palm in the air that demanded for her to hush. She couldn't believe his bold rudeness but she never got a chance to voice her opinion.

AMBER SKY
A.R. DASH

It was Chances turn to speak.

"Now-like I was saying-what you are doing to me is no different than what they do to you. Whether you choose to accept it or not is completely up to you... And to answer your *'simple'* question about what it was to make me change; no I didn't lose a girlfriend; and just for the record, I've never met a woman that I thought was worth my heart. Until I met you. But again, I guess I was wrong...

Anyway, the person who I lost was my grandmother. I was out here fooling around in these streets and I messed around and got into some trouble and I ended up in jail for a while. Well, I was all that my grandmother had; I did everything for her: cooked, cleaned, did the laundry and anything else that she needed me to do. So when I went away, there was nobody left to help her out. A couple of weeks after I went away, social services stopped by to check on her and found her lying in the middle of the living room, unconscious. She had fallen and there was no one there to help her up... she laid there for four days before help came... Now she's gone... And that's how the story ends."

Guilt washed over Sky. Not sure as to what had just happened, she pulled her shades off of her head.

"I'm sorry... I didn't mean---"

He shook his head.

"No...Please don't be sorry...Don't do that. You have nothing to be sorry for. Now if you don't mind, please let me finish."

She didn't interrupt him again. But she stood at the edge of the porch feeling horrible.

"Well when the news reached me, I lost it, I flipped out on a couple of guys in the jail, and by the time the altercation was over, I had nineteen stitches across my face."

He reached up and touched the cut. Sky looked down at Lilly wishing that she would wake up so that she would have a reason to escape his accusing eyes. But that didn't happen. Lilly continued to sleep and Sky was forced to hear the rest of chances story.

"After I was cut in my face, instead of lashing out at the world, I calmed down and turned to God for help. I started reading the bible and praying everyday-"

Sky imagined his pain, it sounded like he went through the same pain she went through when she lost her father. The more he spoke, the more she understood him; the more she understood him, the more she wanted to run down the stairs and to give him a hug as an apology for choosing him to be the one that she lashed out on. She wanted badly for him to forgive her, but couldn't bring herself to ask. And as he stared up at her, guilt gathered in her heart to the point where she looked away from him. She turned away just long enough to make eye contact with the older man that was mowing his lawn. He was done and now sitting in a rocking chair on his porch sipping a cold drink and looking more his age.

The old man greeted Sky with a slight nod of his head and a quick smile. She returned the same greeting, but there was no way of getting away from Chance.

"---To make a long story short. I've been out of jail for about two months and I've been living up to the promises that I made to myself and to God. But I can't lie, times are hard for me right now and temptation is definitely knocking at my door. Especially with the company I keep."

After hearing his story, Sky couldn't for the life of her figure out why he continued to be around people like Dustin.

She had to Ask.

"So why do you still hang out with the same crowd?"

Chance let out a laugh. Then he took his fingers and shaped them like a gun and pretended to shoot himself in the head.

"Pow." He joked. *"I guess I need a hole in my head."*

She quickly agreed. *"I guess you do, because those guys are something else."*

"I know. And you are right. But like I said. I haven't been home for too long and everything is still fresh to me. I tried locking myself up in my small apartment to keep away from everybody, but it felt like the walls were starting to close in on me so I had to get out."

Sky thought about how she always kept herself locked in her room and away from the world and she wanted to tell him that she could relate , but she didn't, she just listened empathetically.

"What I needed was to get out of the house and away from all of the memories. The thing is that those guys were the only-" he put his hands up and made quotations. *"-friends that I had."*

Sky's mouth responded with words before her mind could register what she was saying.

"Why didn't you just go to church or something?"

Her question appeared to catch him off guard.

"I-I-I don't know."

For the next couple of seconds there was a silence. Then he spoke again.

"Don't get me wrong, I have thought a lot about going to church but the thing is, I think I will look like a fool. You see, I am twenty-nine years old and I've never been inside of a Church."

Sky's mouth fell open.

"You have never been inside of a Church?"

Chance shook his head from side to side with a growing embarrassment in his eyes. Sky felt a need to comfort him.

"Well let me be the first to tell you that when it comes to Church, your age doesn't matter. Church welcomes any and every one. Maybe you should really consider going one day."

"You sound like you have some experience." He smiled. *"Maybe you should take me one day."*

This time Sky was the one caught off guard. All she could do was blink.

"Umm... Well umm...."

Sky's mind raced for something to say. They were talking about Church and the last thing she wanted to do was to lie. But the truth of the matter was that she hadn't been inside of the walls of a Church since she moved to Jersey City. Her next thought was that maybe Church was what she needed to get away from some of her own madness. Then she made a mental promise to herself that she would soon go to Church. The question was, would she be willing to bring Chance along with her.

But he was a stranger; and not only that, but he was also a friend of Dustin's. She tried to convince herself that no one should be denied the opportunity to go to Church and then she looked into his face and saw something that touched her deeply. *'What could it hurt?'*.

And then, from the corner of her eye, she saw a vehicle slowing down as it approached her house. She raised her head and saw Josh's car and her heart jumped, then her body locked up. Her mind was arrested with fear and she stood as stiff as a board. The car stopped directly in front of her house, and Josh looked directly into her face. He didn't look like himself. His shirt was messy and he had a face full of unshaved hair. He stared at her with dark black beady eyes.

A shiver started in her legs and traveled through her entire body. She felt an urge to run but she knew she couldn't leave her sister on the porch.

Chance's eyes followed Sky's and he turned his head towards the street. Then he looked back up at Sky and must've read the fear in her face because he turned his entire body towards the street to face Josh as if he was willing to protect her.

Josh pointed a threatening finger at Sky then he slammed on the gas.

'Screeech!!!'

The tires burned rubber and smoke rose from the concrete as the car fish tailed up the block.

Sky's neighbor jumped up out of his rocking chair and pumped his fist into the air while screaming at the runaway vehicle.

Lilly woke up screaming. Her cries sent a shock wave of reality surging through Sky that gave her the strength she needed to move.

She reached down and literally snatched Lilly out of the baby chair. She had to get her into the house where it was safe at. A fear of not knowing what Josh was capable of filled her mind and made her move faster. She adjusted Lilly in one arm then scooped up the baby chair with her free hand.

She'd completely forgotten about Chance until he spoke.

"Hey, is everything okay?"

Sky had the front door open and already had one foot inside of the house.

"Yes...umm. Everything is fine but I have to get going."

Chance took two steps up the stairs.

"Do you need me to stay with you?"

He looked up and down the street like he was looking for Josh's car. Sky quickly considered his offer and truly wanted to accept it but she didn't. Her mother would probably blow her top if she was to come home and find Sky with a man inside of her house. It wouldn't matter that he was Dustin's friend.

Sky declined his offer kindly and ended the conversation by giving him her phone number.

"You don't have to stay here with me, I will be just fine. My mother and everyone should be home shortly... But give me a call sometime okay."

Chance pulled out a small phone and logged in Sky's number. Then she closed the door tightly and locked it behind her.

Inside of the house, Sky paced the living room floor feeding Lilly a bottle in an attempt to put her back to sleep.

*

Almost an hour had passed and her nerves were still a wreck. Sky wondered how many other times Josh had rode pass her house. *'Is he stalking me?'*

She thought to call the police but the truth was that Josh hadn't done nothing wrong; nothing except for scare her half to death.

Lilly fell back asleep and Sky placed laid her on the couch and hoped that her mother would be home soon.

AMBER SKY
A.R. DASH

Sky continued to pace and her steps took her into the
direction of the window. With a gentle tug, She eased back
the curtain and saw Chance sitting on the steps. At first she
wondered why he hadn't left, and then it hit her like a ton of
bricks. Chance had known that she was in the house alone and
he stayed outside to make sure she was okay.

Her heart swelled to capacity and she remembered the
words he's spoken in the kitchen. *'I'd protect you from all of
the uglys in the world'.*

She spoke in a whisper. *"Awww... how sweet... he really
meant what he'd said."*

Silently she watched Chance for a few more minutes, then
her mother's S.U.V. pulled up to the curb. Dustin got out. He
and Chance shook hands and then, without much
conversation, Chance left.

By the time everyone came into the house, Sky was in her
room with the door open and Lilly fast asleep.

Autumn came strolling into her room licking on an ice
cream cone and looking like she felt a whole lot better than
she did earlier.

"So what did the doctor say?" asked Sky.

Autumn stopped licking her ice cream and shrugged her
shoulders.

*"Nothing happened. We sat in the waiting for a while,
Dustin got tired of waiting, and so we left and went to get
some ice cream."*

The words were like a physical blow.

"What do you mean, Dustin got tired of waiting?"

171

AMBER SKY
A.R. DASH

Autumn shut down as if she was being accused of some wrong doing and she looked into Sky's face like she was intimidated.

Dustin and Charlene came walking pass Sky's room door. Sky shot a look out of the door that caused her mother to stop short.

Her mother looked at her dumbfounded.

"What's the matter with you?"

"Why didn't you wait for her to see a doctor?"

Charlene's response was cool.

"I got tired of sitting in that waiting room around all of those germy people. And besides, she feels better anyhow. Don't you Autumn?"

Autumn looked like she was afraid to answer. And then she looked at Sky with weak eyes and nodded her head up and down.

Sky wanted to make the argument that just because Autumn felt better at the moment, didn't mean that there wasn't anything wrong with her. But Sky kept her thoughts to herself. Instead, she picked Lilly up off of the bed and walked over to her mother and handed her the baby. Then she turned her back to her mother and mumbled.

"This is just sad."

Nobody else said anything and then Charlene and Autumn left Sky in the room by herself. Sky closed the door and laid across her bed wondering how long it was going to be until she figured out how to go about getting public assistance.

AMBER SKY
A.R. DASH

CHAPTER 13.

A few restless hours later, Sky woke up to the sound of her ringing phone. Her first thought was that it had to be either Josh or Danielle.

She reached over to her nightstand and picked up her phone to look at the screen. The caller wasn't calling private but the number wasn't familiar to her. She cleared her throat, and thinking that it might still be one of them, she answered in a bothered tone.

"Hello?"

"Yes, hello, umm, Sky..."

"Yes this is Sky... Who's calling?"

The voice came to life.

"This is Chance."

Sky sat up and swung her feet to the floor. She had to gather her thoughts. At first she didn't recall giving him her number then the incident from earlier rushed her mind as if it had just happened.

"Oh Chance. How are you doing?"

"I'm okay... But the question is, how are you doing?"

She knew that he was referring to what had taken place with Josh and a vision of Josh speeding up the street like a speed demon gave Sky some worry that she really didn't feel like dealing with. She tried her best to re-direct the conversation but Chance wouldn't let her.

"I'm okay. Just a little tire, that's all."

Chance let a silence fall between them for a split second before he continued.

"Hey Sky... I know that it may be none of my business but you looked anything but okay earlier. I've been thinking about

what happened all day and I have been really worried about you."

Sky enjoyed his sincerity.

"I appreciate your concern but really, I'm okay... you don't have to worry yourself... Especially on my account."

"It's a little late for that Amber Sky. But I can't help but to wonder... is that guy the reason why you have that bruise on your face."

It was like being struck by lightning. She looked in the mirror at the fading bruise and really didn't know what to say. The truth was that, yes, Josh was the reason why she had that bruise, but Chance probably thought that Josh had put his hands on her.

"Uh, No... No, he didn't put his hands on me if that's what you are thinking."

"Hmmm." Replied Chance.

His response made Sky think that he didn't believe her.

"Listen Chance, like I said, I appreciate your concern, I really do. But I m a big girl and I can handle myself."

"Um-hmm... I Agree. You are a big girl, but this is a ugly world, and some things, even big girl shouldn't have to deal with."

He was right.

"Do you mind if I ask you who that guy was?"

Sky hesitated. And in her moment of hesitation, the whole scene with Josh pulling up to her house played out differently. In the vision, Josh jumped out of his car and him and Chance got into a big fist fight in the middle of the street. She knew that that is how it would have played out because there was no doubt in her mind that Chance would have stood up for her.

Her vision made her believe that the least she could do was be honest with him.

"Chance listen... I am going to tell you the truth because that is the only thing that I know how to do. I don't know why, but I feel like that truth is what you deserve. So please... Just bear with me."

"Amber Sky." he said in a tender voice. *"Not only will I bear with you, but I will be here for you if that is what you need... I am willing to listen to you for as long as you need to talk."*

And that is exactly what they did. Sky talked and Chance listened. She told him about what happened between herself, Josh and Danielle, and then she told him about the undying love she had for her siblings and how she was trying to move them out of her mother's house.

He listened as she poured her heart out about the love/hate relationship she had with her mother and she even cried as she told him about what Dustin had done to her.

They stayed on the phone for hours and along with all of the things that she disliked about her life, she also told him about her dreams and goals and how one day she planned to move away to Hawaii, open up Tiki Bar and buy a house ten minutes away from the beach that overlooked the mountains.

In return, she gave Chance the floor and he opened up and told her about the goods, the bads and the uglys in his life and he even told her that he would help her get her siblings out of that house.

Sky felt like she could talk to and listen to him forever.

It was amazing. And after they talked, Chance didn't come around to see Dustin anymore because of what he had done to Sky.

Over the next few weeks, he and Sky spoke over the phone regularly. And in that time, a bond was created that only death could separate.

CHAPTER 14.

Sky sat on the edge of the tub while the hot shower ran. Steam from the shower clouded the bathroom and Sky thought deeply about Chance.

For the past three weeks, she spent practically every waking moment talking to him on the phone. The conversations went well and although they seemed to have a natural connection, she still kept him at a safe distance.

He would ask her if he could come to see her, or if they could meet at a park or something like that, but she always made up an excuse why she had no time to see him.

"I really would like to see you Chance but I have a job interview." She would say. Or, *"I have an appointment at the welfare office."* She would confess shamefully.

Fortunately for her, he was not judgmental. After hearing what went on at the house of horrors, he actually encouraged her to apply for some kind of governmental assistance so that she could get out of her mother's house quicker.

But for Sky, the process was just too much. The welfare office had her jumping through loop after loop after loop, and she still hadn't gotten any help.

Chance was very supportive and continued to cheer her on and finally, after some strong self-convincing, Sky felt as though Chance had earned a date with her.

"I think I'm ready to go out with you." Were her exact words.

*

Sky stepped into the shower and the pressure of the piping hot water revived her tense body. *'What am I about to do?'* She asked the silent angels around her. *'He seems like a really nice guy, but he admitted himself that he used to be just like Dustin and the rest of them. What if he really hasn't changed?*

AMBER SKY
A.R. DASH

What am I going to do then? I still have time, so maybe I should just call the whole thing off.'

Sky closed her eyes and put her face under the steaming water and weighed both sides of the situation. On one side she had a guy named Chance who brought with him a not so friendly past and on the other hand she had a guy named Chance who had played the cards he was dealt in life, and from a moral stand point, he'd come out on top.

The conclusion she came too was that everyone has a past and as far as she was concerned, he'd proven himself worthy of her friendship.

But there was one more thing to consider; and that was the fact that not only had she agreed to go out with him, but neither one of them really had any money, so she agreed to go over to his apartment to watch a couple of movies with him. *'Please Lord let him be on his best behavior'.*

'What am I doing?' The question continued to haunt her.

With two hours left, she unwrapped the towel from around her body then looked down at the dress she was supposed to have worn to Josh's so-called nephew's party. Hopefully, it wouldn't be to over the top for him.

It took her every minute of the two hours to get herself to the point where she was pleased with how she looked. And then she stepped over to the full length mirror to admire herself. She was stunning.

The vanilla cream strapless dress hugged every curve of her body with class. The bottom of the dress stopped just above her knees giving life to her tone legs and made her calves look nice and thick.

Her sun kissed skin held a glow and also appeared to be sprinkled with some type of spritsy glitter. Her rusty red hair was pulled into a tight bun that sat perfectly in the back of her head and helped to bring out every feature of her beautiful face. And as usual, her lips were covered by her shiny strawberry lip gloss.

The only Jewelry she wore was an ankle bracelet that she'd had for years. When she was putting it on, she thought about her butterfly pendant and wondered if Danielle or Josh had found it.

Sky really hoped that she wasn't too overdressed for a simple movie date. But as her dad always told her *'You only get one chance to make a first impression'*.

She was ready to go so she picked up her phone and dialed Chances number.

After a nervous two rings, she heard his voice.

"Hello?"

"Hey Chance, it's me, Sky."

"Hey Amber Sky, how are you?"

She smiled when he said her name but wondered if her father was jealous. The thought passed and she took joy from the fact that she liked to hear him say it.

"I'm doing fine Chance, thanks for asking. I was just calling to let you know that I would be leaving shortly for your house. Actually, as soon as I get off of the phone with you I am going to call an Uber. I was just calling because I wanted to make sure that I had the right address. Hold on a minute, let me grab it."

"Okay."

Sky reached into the little purse that she would be carrying and she pulled out a folded up piece of paper. She opened it and then put the phone back to her ear.

"Chance?"

"Yeah I'm still here."

"The address is 42 Armstrong Avenue, is that correct?"

"Yes that is correct. But don't forget, the entrance to my apartment is on the side of the house."

"I won't. Just let me call an Uber and I should be seeing you short---"

"Hold on... Hold on for a minute."

"Yes Chance?"

"Well I was just wondering... Umm... Do you mind if I order some pizza to go along with the movie? As I told you, I don't have much of a menu here."

"No I don't mind at all Chance... But can I have mushrooms please?"

"Ewww... you eat mushrooms?"

Sky laughed.

"Doesn't everybody?"

"Nooo... I have never tried them."

"Well you should. Trust me, you won't regret it."

"Pssst... aww what the heck. 'YOLO' You only live once right? A large pie with mushrooms it is."

The gesture was a small but it touched Sky in a big way.

"Thank you Chance, YOLO... And I will see you in a little while okay?"

"No problem Amber Sky... I will be waiting."

AMBER SKY
A.R. DASH

Armstrong Avenue was a fifteen minute ride away. Sky paid the driver, got out of the car and found herself standing in front of a fenced in blue two family house. She looked across the yard and the numbers on the door confirmed that she was at the right address. But she reached into her purse for the folded up piece of paper anyway.

Sky looked at the paper, then up at the door, then she walked up to the gate. *'Well here goes nothing girl'*. She reached out and unlocked the gate then entered the yard.

There was no turning back. She was just steps away from being alone with Chance. Without warning, her stomach tightened and her nerves came to life.

Shy took a couple of deep breaths then balled her hands into fist a couple of times and was able to calm herself.

She looked up at the house.

All of the curtains were drawn shut. It gave the house a sense of privacy. Like whoever lived there didn't care to be bothered by the outside world. Sky looked around the yard and didn't remember asking Chance if there were any dogs on the property. But she thought she was sure that if there were any, he would have told her about it.

She walked with light steps just to be safe and took a brick laid path that led to the side of the house and she searched for Chance's door.

On the side of the house there were three neatly stacked trash bags. Other than that, it was an empty alley.

As she walked along the side of the house, she hoped that Chances nice ways weren't a cover up for some crazy hidden life style that he lived.

A quick vision of him charging at her with his mouth open exposing Vampire fangs flashed through her mind and she laughed it off. Then she stopped walking and pulled her cell phone out and put 911 on speed dial. *'You could never be to safe'*. She told herself.

Some stairs leading down to a white door came into view and she knew that she'd reached her destination. *'It's show time'*.

She looked up to the bright Sky and thought about her father. *'Daddy I know that you're with me'*.

After saying a short prayer she took careful steps down the few stairs. Her four inch heals clicked. There was a little round bell along the door panel so she reached out and pressed it and heard a ding dong sound. Shortly after, there were footsteps approaching the door.

Sky held her breath and didn't know what to hope for or if she should hope for anything at all. She felt a sudden case of the jitters but knew that she couldn't back out if she wanted too. Everything began to move in slow motion.

First she heard the click of the lock being undone, then she saw the doorknob turning. She let out three hard breaths really quick and then Chance pulled the door open.

Chance froze with his mouth hanging open. His eyes paused as he stared at Sky in obvious astonishment. Clearly he was beyond pleased with what he saw.

"Wow! You-you-you look amazing."

Sky giggled and the color of blush showed on her cheeks.

"Thank you Chance, you don't look too bad yourself."

He had on a colorful checker board shirt and a pair of blue jeans with a pair of Timberland boots. His dreadlocks were freshly done and pulled back into a ponytail. His goatee was razor sharp and Sky had to resist the urge to reach out and touch the scar on his face.

"Thank you Sky, I appreciate the compliment."

He stood there holding the door open and she could tell that he was completely overcome by her from the lost look in his eyes.

Playfully she waved her hand in front of his face and giggled.

"Hello... Hello... is anyone home?"

Chance snapped out of his moment of awe and let out and embarrassing laugh.

"I'm sorry, where are my manners? Please come inside."

He backed up to make room for her and she crossed the threshold into Chance's world.

It was just as small as he described it to be, if not smaller. The entire apartment was made up of one square space about as big as an oversized bedroom. There was one window. A mall square on the left wall that did little when it came to brightening the place up. The main source of light came from a bulb hanging from a wire in the middle of the room. The floor was covered by little white square tiles and the cleanliness of them gave the place a bright and fresh feeling.

Over in the far corner of the room there was a twin size bed. It was neatly made with a single pillow on top of it and the sheets were pulled so tight that it looked like a quarter could bounce off of the bed.

Then, in the middle of the room, under the hanging bulb, there was a two cushion love seat and in front of it, Chance had a twenty-seven inch T.V. and a D.V.D. player sitting on top of a T.V. stand and a fold away closet and a bin was in another corner.

Finally, against an unfinished wall of wooden beams was Chances kitchen. A mini refrigerator and a picnic table with a microwave oven on top of it. Sitting next to the microwave was stack of dishes. Sky didn't see a sink, so she assumed the bathroom to be where he cleaned them.

Although he had forewarned her about the place, it was still a bit much to take in, but overall, Sky felt that she really couldn't have a judgment because Chance's apartment might not have been the most luxurious, but at least he had somewhere to call his own.

Chance stood behind her and she could feel him watching her as she observed her surroundings.

She turned around and looked into his face. His handsome smile showed no signs of shame or embarrassment.

"I told you that the place was small."

"Yes you did."

She could tell that he was in high spirits so she decided to do a little joking herself.

"So now that the grand tour is over, what exactly do you have planned for us?"

He put a finger up to his chin.

"Hmmm... let me see, how does this sound... I was thinking that we could continue to get to know each other for the first year; work on our dreams and goals the second year; save up some money the third year; and then get married, have children and spend the rest of our lives together."

"Awww, that was sweet."

"No but seriously." He rolled his hand then bowed his head and began to speak in a royal accent.

"If you don't mind Madam, would you please follow me this way?"

He took her by the hand and led her over to the loveseat. Then he fluffed the cushions and continued to speak as if he was her servant.

"And this is where the Madam will be entertained for the evening."

Sky found his role playing to be cute so she joined in on his game.

"Why thank you kind sir."

They shared an ice breaking laugh then Chance walked over to the T.V. stand and picked up three D.V.D.s.

He walked back over and handed them to Sky.

"This will be tonight's movie selection. I hope that Madam finds something to her liking. But until then---" He picked up the remote and handed it to her. *"-feel free to enjoy some of the finest basic cable television that this side of town has to offer."*

"Thank you." Said she replied and then she took hold of the remote.

Sky found herself really enjoying Chance's company and she was now happy that she had come over. From the corner of her eyes, she saw a shadow pass the small window and shortly after the doorbell rang. Quickly she looked at Chance.

"No need for alarm, that is only the pizza delivery man. I shall return shortly."

He walked away with his head held high and his shoulders square; like he was a man sure of himself.

Sky liked what she saw. She smiled behind his back and then let her attention fall to the three movies. The selection warmed her heart: Beauty and the beast, The Titanic and The Notebook.

AMBER SKY
A.R. DASH

His choices earned him some cool points with her and showed her that he had a sensitive side that he was in touch with. Sky could have never imagined watching any of the movies with Josh and the thought of him left a bad taste in her mouth. Chance came back carrying a box of pizza and he sat it next to the microwave.

Sky took the remote and pretended to flip through the channels, but in reality she was watching Chance maneuver around his small kitchen.

It was late in the afternoon on a Thursday. Sky hadn't made up her mind as to just how long she planned on staying, so she told herself that if the evening continued to go as well as it was going, then she would stay and watch all three of the movies.

Chance opened the box and the aroma of pizza filled the air and caused Sky's stomach to rumble. She hadn't eaten all day. Her stomach rumbled a second time and she hoped that Chance didn't hear it. But he did.

He lifted his head from what he was doing and sent her a smile without saying anything. Sky felt blood rush to her cheeks and she blushed with embarrassment.

When Chance was done in the kitchen area, he came walking over to Sky balancing two plates and two cans of Dr. Pepper sodas. He handed Sky one of the plates while making a playfully disgusted face.

"Mushrooms, as the lady requested."

Sky twisted her face as if she agreed with the feeling he was having. "Thank you." She took the plate and stood up. "Do you mind if I use your rest room? I need to clean myself up."

"No I don't mind at all. Go right ahead."

He took the plate back from her hand and sat everything down.

"Right this way."

He led her to the bathroom and stopped at the entrance.

Sky spoke graciously.

"Thank you."

She went into the bathroom and closed the door behind her. She washed her hands and checked her face and then turned off the faucet. She was about to leave the bathroom but something told her to open up the medicine cabinet. She didn't even second guess herself.

She pulled open the mirror and the first thing she saw was a small brown medicine bottle.

"Hmmm..." she mumbled.

Then she picked the bottle up and began reading the label. It was prescribed to Chance and from what she could see, the medicine was some kind of sleep aid medication. Suddenly, she felt like she was invading his privacy so she put the pills back and rushed out of the bathroom.

Chance was sitting in front of the T.V. already halfway done with a slice of mushroom topped pizza. He looked up at Sky with grease all over his lips and hands.

"I'm sorry, but I couldn't wait, I haven't eaten anything all day... By the way, these mushrooms are delicious."

The shared a genuine laugh and Sky dove for her plate.

"I feel your pain because I haven't eaten all day either-" She stuffed her mouth with a big bite. *"-but I told you that you'd like mushrooms."*

She sat down next to him and ate like it was her last meal

Chance put his plate down and turned to Sky.

"So have you decided what movie you want to watch?"

"Yes I have... if you don't mind, I would like to watch the Notebook. I haven't seen it, but I hear that it's really good."

Chance got excited.

"You've never seen it! Great! You're going to love it. I'm promise you... It's probably the greatest love story ever."

He put the movie in and then turned off the light and sat next to her. His mild scented soap took hold of Sky and she made a mental note to see what kind of soap he used.

The light from the television laminated the room and gave the place a warm feeling. Sky and Chance *'Awwwed* throughout the whole movie. Next he put in The Titanic, but the talked through the entire movie about The Notebook and how powerful one man's love was for his dying wife.

Sky had never met anyone like Chance. She felt as if something was magnetically pulling them together. His company was to die for. When she talked, he really listened and in return she did the same. He showed interest and respect for her every opinion even if he didn't agree with it. And not only was he fun to be around, but he knew how to be serious when the occasion called for it.

Sky poured out her heart because talking to him came natural. It was her first time talking to him face to face about Josh or Dustin or about anything for that matter, so when she spoke, she spoke with so much passion that her heart swelled and her tears welled.

As she told him about all of the heartache that she'd been faced with andshe saw a growing fire in Chances eyes as he listened to her. It was obvious that he was bothered by hearing about what was done to her, but he kept himself under control.

Sky got extra emotional as she told him about Dustin and in the middle of one of her sentences, Chance took his index finger and placed it softly over her lips to calm her.

"Shhhh..." he whispered.

The dim light from the T.V. made them look like silhouettes. The beautiful song at the end of The Titanic played and the way Chance looked into Sky's eyes gave her a feel of comfort.

His voice was low but manly.

"You don't ever have to go through any of that pain again... You deserve so much more. Right now I can't offer you much, but the one thing I can offer for certain, is protection from the ugly things that you have seen."

Sky looked away from him and he reached out and lightly touched her chin to turn her to face him. She had tears in her eyes. He had care in his.

"I will protect you even if it cost me my life Sky. All you have to do is give me a Chance to be your hero?"

It felt like he was speaking to her heart. She searched his face for signs of deceit but couldn't find any. Her soul was captivated by wonder but her vulnerable eyes ran away from his deep gaze.

Through the speakers of the T.V., Celine Dion sang passionately. She sang about a love that would reach her lover no matter how near or far he was.

Sky wanted that kind of love. She looked back up into Chance's face.

In her mind she was afraid but her heart told her that there was nothing to be afraid of; that this moment was real; that she deserved the feelings she were having; and that the man sitting in front of her, would be there for her no matter what.

She held Chance's gaze and a lonely tear crawled down her face. Her voice was weak.

"Please don't hurt me Chance... Please... my heart can't take any more pain."

Slowly he leaned into her and Sky closed her eyes and leaned into him. Their lips met, and a floodgate of passion was unlocked.

Sky never experienced the type of tenderness and desire Chance showed her. He made her forget about all of her pain and then he took her to his bed and made love to her in a way that she had never known.

What Sky did know was that she had finally found love; and not just any love, but the type of love that people die for.

CHAPTER 15.

Two nights had passed and Sky was still locked within the walls of Chance's basement apartment. Their passion for one another would not allow them to separate.

Late on Saturday afternoon, Sky once again found herself awakening to the safety and protection of Chances arms. Every time she looked at him her heart vibrated.

Together they laid in the bed wrapped in each other's love and talking about the future. As they did so, Chance said something to pierce her with delight.

"How about we get up tomorrow and find ourselves a Church to join?"

His suggestion warmed her entire body. She sat up on her elbows and looked at his relaxed expression.

"Are you serious? I mean, you don't have to go to Church just to impress me."

"Thank you, but that is not why I want to do it. I just really believe that it's time for me to show my appreciation to the Lord."

"That's a very good reason Chance. But you've never been to a Church. Are you sure that you're ready?"

"I believe that I am... I mean... I'm not going to sit here and tell you that I'm not nervous... but with you by my side Amber Sky, I think I can take over the world."

"Awww... You're so sweet..."

She leaned over and gave him a light kiss. Then she remembered that the only clothing she had was the tight fitting dress she'd worn to his house. It was definitely not appropriate for Church.

AMBER SKY
A.R. DASH

It was already about six o'clock, and if Sky wanted to go with Chance the next morning, she would have to get up and go to her mother's house for a change of clothes.

She jumped up and wrapped the sheet around her body and stood over the bed.

"If we're going to Church tomorrow, then I have to go to my mother's house to get a change of clothes."

"Oh yeah... you're right. I will come along with you okay?"

"No problem. I'm going to take a quick shower alright?"

"Okay... I will straighten up a little. Let me know if you need anything."

"I will."

Sky ran into the bathroom and closed the door behind her. Then she turned on the shower, but she didn't get in right away. Instead she stood in front of the mirror looking at herself for a while. She stared at her reflection and wondered about what was happening between her and Chance.

She searched herself for any reasons to undo the things that she'd done with him, but she couldn't find one. Everything about the situation brought joy to her and for the first time in a long time, she looked into the mirror and didn't see a fool staring back at her.

She had happiness written all over her face and there was no way of hiding it.

Her prayers had been answered. Her father must have heard her crying out for someone of her own to love and sent Chance to fill that void.

The steam rose up from the shower and began to fog up the mirror. Sky unwrapped the sheet from her body and let it fall to the floor. She reached out to wipe the fog from the mirror but unconsciously pulled the mirror open and looked into the medicine cabinet again. For a second time she picked up the small bottle of pills and for no reason other than pure curiosity, she twisted off the cap.

The bottle was filled three quarters of the way with little white pills. *'Why does he need pills to help him sleep?'* she asked herself.

Suddenly she heard a light knock on the door that startled her and caused her to drop the open bottle onto the floor. The bottle hit the floor and the pills scattered all over the bathroom. Sky dove to the floor in an attempt to gather them, but they were everywhere.

She scooped up as many as she could but there was no way to get them all, so she let out a deep sigh and stopped trying. Then she stood up and walked over to the door and opened it for Chance. She must have had a nervous facial expression because Chance became alarmed.

He rushed into the bathroom.

"Is everything okay?"

Sky didn't try to lie. She shook her head and told him exactly what had happened. Then she took the almost empty bottle and raised it up to show him what she was talking about.

Her voice was filled with guilt.

"I'm sorry Chance. I really wasn't trying to be nose I-I-I just---"

She really had nothing to say.

Chance looked down at the pills spread all over the floor then he looked at Sky and smiled.

"You Noooossy."

AMBER SKY
A.R. DASH

Sky poked out her bottom lip.

"Please forgive me."

He reached out and gently took the medicine bottle from her hand, then they bent down and picked up the rest of the pills together.

Chance was quiet, and Sky was full of shame. When they were done, they both stood up.

"You are probably wondering why I take these." Said Chance. *"Well, these pills have been my best friend ever since I lost my grandma. After she died, I came down with a terrible sleeping disorder that the doctors said would kill me if I didn't treat it... so they prescribed me these pills-"*

Sky began to feel worse.

"-I've had episodes where I didn't sleep for three and four days at a time... that was until I got my hands on these little babies. All I need is a half of one of these puppies, and I could easily sleep for anywhere from eight to twelve hours."

Then Chance did something shocking.

He twisted the top back onto the medicine bottle and then tossed it into the small trash can at the side of the sink.

Sky was puzzled.

Then he looked at her.

"I don't think that I need them anymore." He reached out and took her naked body into his arms. *"For the past couple of nights that you have been here with me, I haven't taken the pills and I have been sleeping just fine... So unless you plan on going somewhere---"* Playfully he pulled away from her and acted as if he was about to dig the pills out of the trash. *"---then I will keep the pills."*

Sky pulled him back into her arms and spoke from her soul.

"I'm not going anywhere Chance-" His words had touched the core of who she was. She hugged him with all of her strength and spoke truthfully. *"-I promise. I promise to be right here by your side for as long as you allow me to be."*

They stood there holding each other like their lives depended on the firmness of their hug. Then they kissed and Chance joined her in the shower and was gentle with her.

During the shower, not only did they love one another, but they also washed away what was left of one another's pain.

For Sky, it was like being snatched out of nightmare and placed into a fairytale.

They spent more time in the shower than they anticipated and now they had to race against the clock because the last bus leaving towards Sky's mother's house was due to depart in thirty minutes.

Chance finished getting dressed first and he was waiting for Sky to put on her shoes when they heard the sound of a garbage truck outside of the house.

"Aw man! I forgot that tonight is trash night. I have to put the trash out on the curb!"

He dug into his pocket, pulled out a key ring with two keys on it and tossed them to Sky.

"Lock the door behind you! I'm going to try to catch the garbage truck."

Sky caught the keys and stuffed them into her bra. Chance shot out of the house and Sky squeezed her feet into her heels and left out of the house behind him. She stepped outside and was about to lock the door but looked down the alley and saw that there was still one garbage bag still sitting there. An urge to help Chance took over her and she forgot to lock the door. She ran up to the bag and without a second thought, she grabbed it and joined Chance in his effort to catch the truck.

The bag was heavy and smelled terrible but she didn't care. She didn't even care that she had on a pretty dress and high heel shoes. The only thing that she cared about was helping Chance.

She made it to the gate and saw that Chance was able to stop the truck. The two men hanging off of the back of the truck jumped down to help Chance. The first guy took a bag out of Chance's hand then turned around and carried it to the truck. The second guy noticed Sky and walked pass Chance to help her.

Chance turned to see where he was going and when he turned around, he saw Sky dragging a bag that was half her size. He stopped in the middle of the street and just looked at her.

The garbage man took the bag from Sky and came walking back towards Chance.

"Looks like you got yourself somebody that's going to help you out with any and everything that life throws your way."

All Chance could do was smile.

"I know... Believe me, I know."

Chance threw the bag into the back of the truck then he walked over to Sky and thanked her with a big kiss. Both of the garbage men stopped their duties and watched as the couple walked hand and hand towards the bus stop.

Sky and Chance made it to the bus stop with time to spare. They snuggled against each other and talked for about ten minutes before the bus arrived. A short ride later, they were getting off of the bus and walking down the street of the house of horrors...

From the moment Sky stepped off of the bus, she felt like she was stepping further and further away from her fairytale and back into the harsh nightmare that was her life. The closer she got to her mother's house the more she realized just how much she disliked the place.

To get her mind off of her unwanted thoughts, she looked up at Chance from under his arm and started making small talk.

"So what do you think about bringing my sister's to Church with us?"

"Sounds like a great idea. But truthfully, I think that we should get ourselves established in a Church before we bring them along."

"That makes sense."

Sky's mind was not fully on the conversation. She was too busy looking around a neighborhood that she'd grown to dislike with a passion. Even the air near her mother's house seemed gloomier than anywhere else. Back at the bus stop near Chance's house, the air was warm and inviting, now the air held an uncomfortable chill.

Her body grew tense and unconsciously she held on tighter to Chance.

Lights were barely on throughout the neighborhood and there was not a single person outside. Sky looked around for her mother's S.U.V. but didn't see it. That meant that her mother had gone to work and Dustin had driven her…

A feeling of relief came over her that loosened the tightness she felt between her shoulders. But the thought of her mother and Dustin not being home was a bitter sweet thought because more than likely, Autumn was stuck babysitting again. *'We'll be out of there soon Autumn. Don't worry.* Sky thought as she walked comfortably in Chance's arms. *'Now I have someone to help me'*.

AMBER SKY
A.R. DASH

Sky and Chance approached the house and Sky quickly reached into her purse and pulled out the keys. She hoped Autumn was sleep because she wanted to be in and out of the house as soon as possible. And plus she didn't want to see the look on Autumn's face when she left back out.

Sky opened the door and allowed Chance to enter first.

The lights in the living room were turned off and the house was quiet except for the sound of a television that was coming from one of the rooms in the back. Sky knew that more than likely it was Autumn in her room watching T.V. with Lilly.

Sky walked through the kitchen with Chance right behind her. She looked over to the sink where she'd been standing when Chance made the comment about protecting her from all of the uglys in the world and her heart smiled.

She couldn't help but to turn around and look into his face. He was also smiling. His thoughts must've been the same as hers, but neither one of them said anything. And they didn't have too. The way they looked at each other told a story that words would have only ruined.

"Wait right here Chance, I'll be right back."

Chance stopped in the doorway of the kitchen and nodded his head. Sky turned away from him and continued to walk down the short hallway that led to her room. The sound of the television was coming from her room and she knew that that was where Autumn was at.

She opened her room door and felt a sledge hammer hit her in her chest.

Dustin was standing in the middle of her bedroom with his pants down to his ankles and a beer bottle hanging from his hand and Autumn down on her knees in front of him doing the unthinkable.

Sky screamed like a wild animal and charged into the room.

"Ahhhh!!!"

She went at Dustin with her arms swinging wildly.

Dustin spun around with a surprised look on his face and pushed Autumn down to the floor. Autumn let out a loud cry. Dustin wrestled to pull his pants up without letting go of the beer bottle.

Sky got close enough to him to land an open handed smack. It had no effect. Dustin raised the beer bottle into the air and brought it crashing down against the side of Sky's head.

'Smash!'

The bottle shattered on impact and the blow sent Sky stumbling to the floor with a painful cry.

"Ughhh!"

Chance jumped into the doorway. *"You son of a bitch!"* He charged at Dustin.

Dustin had his pants up and braced himself for Chance's attack. Chance swung a wild punch. Dustin blocked it and they grabbed each other in a life or death struggle. Chance fought hard, but so did Dustin. They exchanged powerful blows to each other's heads and Sky laid on the floor clutching the side of her face. Blood seeped through her fingers and she tried to shake off her daze. Autumn screamed frantically.

"Ahhhhh!—Ahhhhh!—Ahhhhh!"

Outside of Sky's window a neighbor turned on their lights.

Chance was on top of Dustin Choking him but somehow Dustin wrestled his way to his feet and gave Chance a hard shove backwards. Chance stumbled and tripped over Autumn and he slammed into the dresser then his body crashed to the floor.

Autumn screamed louder.

"AHHHHHH!!!"

From one of the other rooms, Lilly started crying.

Dustin took off running from Sky's room in a drunken stumble. Chance jumped up breathing heavily and shot out of the room behind him. Sky's blurry vision came too just in time to see Chance's body bend the corner and she screamed out.

"Chance!!!"

Lilly was still screaming hysterically. Sky jumped up and ran over to Autumn and pulled her up from the floor.

"Go Get Lilly! Go and get her!"

She pushed Autumn towards the door then ran into the living room. She didn't see Chance or Dustin anywhere, but the front door was wide open. Sky wiped away a trickle of blood from her eye then she shot out of the house like a bolt of lightning.

The neighborhood that was just empty, was now filled with almost everyone who lived there and everybody watched as Dustin and Chance wrestled in the middle of the street over a baseball bat. Sky's old lawn mowing neighbor came running up to her and grabbed her by the shoulders.

"What happen? What happen?"

Sky shouted hysterically.

"He raped my sister!!! He raped her!!!"

Wailing sirens came speeding up the block and the police cruiser stopped right in front of the brawl. A police officer

jumped out just as Chance won the struggle over the bat.
Chance had murder in his eyes.

The cop drew his weapon.

"Freeze!"

Dustin laid flat on his back in the middle of the street and held
his arms up defensively in anticipation of a blow. Chance
cocked the bat back wildly over his head and let out a savage
scream.

"HHHAAA!!!"

With a powerful swing, he brought the bat down violently
against Dustin's head. The sound was horrific.

"Thump!"

The officer shouted.

"Drop the weapon! Drop the weapon!"

Chance was too zoned out to hear him. He cocked the bat back
a second time.

Sky watched the whole scene in slow motion. She yelled
towards the cop.

"Noooo!!!"

Her screams fell on deaths ears.

Dustin laid spread out on the ground not moving and Chance
let out another savage scream.

"HHHAAAA!!!"

The cop was forced to pull the trigger.

"POW!!!"

The shot echoed and the bullet slammed into the middle of Chance's chest. His body stiffened, he dropped the bat, and then he fell on top of Dustin.

The crowd dispersed.

Sky yelled. *"Channnce!!!"*

She pulled away from her neighbor and took off running for Chance. When she reached him, she bent down and cuffed his head into her arms. He was already coughing up blood.

She looked around crazily.

"Call an ambulance!!! Please!!! Somebody call an ambulance!!!"

She looked down at Chance and saw nothing but fear in his eyes. He looked like he knew he was dying. He coughed and blood bubbled in his mouth and then trailed down his cheek.

"Stay with me Chance... Stay with me Chance... Please stay with me."

He tried to speak, but gagged on his blood. Sky knew she was losing him.

"Save your energy baby... Don't try to talk."

She held his head and looked around helplessly.

"Help me!!! Please!!! Somebody help me!!!"

One of the cops ran up and stood over them.

"An ambulance is on the way!"

And then she heard Chance's voice.

"Am-Amber, Amber Sky."

AMBER SKY
A.R. DASH

She looked down into his face. He tried to force a smile at the corner of his mouth.

Sky answered him in a small and friendly voice.

"Yes Chance... I'm right here baby... I'm right here."

She could see the life fading from his eyes. Looking at him was too much but there was no way that she was going to look away from him. An eternity passed as they held each other's gaze and Chance dedicated his last breath to her.

"I told you that I would protect you even if it cost me my life... Amber Sky, I love yo---"

The life left from his eyes and his head dangled to one side.

A river of tears fell down Sky's face.

"Channnnnce!!!"

He died in Sky's arms before she had the chance to tell him that she loved him. The Ambulance came and picked his body up and Sky rode in the back of a cop car with Autumn and Lilly to the hospital.

*

At the hospital, the police had questions for Autumn and the doctors had to run test on her but they could do nothing until Charlene got there.

Sky sat numbly with her arm around Autumn. How could she let this happen to her sister? Her heart was heavy. Sky realized that all the signs were there; Autumn not wanting Sky to stay out all night; Sky waking up in the middle of the night to find Autumn curled up underneath her... and there were other things that she knew she should have paid more attention too.

Sky sat in the hospital room numb with pain.

AMBER SKY
A.R. DASH

Charlene came running into the room towards Sky with a guilty face.

"What Happened?"

Sky couldn't look at her. Sky stood up and walked pass her mother like she was a complete stranger.

Once she got outside she kept walking and walking and walking. She walked until she found herself in front of Chances house. She realized that she hadn't locked the door so she went inside.

Sky looked around the small apartment and the tears started to fall. She walked into the bathroom and stared into the mirror and cried and cried and cried. She had failed miserably. Not only herself, but she had also failed Autumn, Danielle and Chance as well. The pain was too much to bear and she didn't want to deal with it anymore.

She put the toilet seat down and was about to sit but noticed the bottle of sleeping pills. She reached down into the small trash can and grabbed them. Then she bawled like a baby and called out for her father.

"I don't want to be here no more Daddy! Please forgive me!"

She twisted the cap off of the pill bottle and poured a bunch of pills into her hand. It was about twenty eight pills in all. Chance only needed a half of one to sleep for twelve hours but Sky was about to shove twenty eight into her mouth hoping that she would never wake up again.

"Daddy!!!"

She raised her hand and opened her mouth.

Then she squeezed her eyes as tight as she could and an image of Autumn popped into her head.

"Autumn!" She cried out loud. *"My sister needs me--- What am I doing."*

Autumn still needed her. She could feel it. She jumped up and let all of the pills fall from her hand.

"I have to get back to the hospital."

Sky turned around and ran out of Chance's apartment and ran as hard as she could. She ran for Chance and she ran for her father; but more importantly, she ran for Autumn.

When she reached the hospital, the first thing she saw was her mother crying and being led away in hand cuffs.

Sky ran up to her. *"Where is Autumn! Where is Lilly!"*

"I'm sorry Sky... I'm so sorry..."

Sky didn't understand what was going on.

"Where is Autumn! Where are they at?"

The cop stepped in between them and pointed.

"Your siblings are in that room with a social service worker."

Sky ran for the room. Autumn was sitting on a table crying like crazy and a white lady was standing in front of her trying to talk to her.

Autumn looked up and saw Sky.

"Sky!"

She jumped down and ran into her sister's arms. Sky had returned just before the social service worker took the children into the states custody.

Sky and Autumn latched onto each other and stood in the middle of the room crying.

AMBER SKY
A.R. DASH

*

CONCLUSION:

A week had passed and Sky sat in disbelief with an open newspaper. Autumn and Lilly were in her room asleep.

Dustin's crime against Autumn became state wide news. His picture was in every newspaper throughout the state. Alongside of his picture, there was also a picture of Charlene. She was also charge with a crime.

Apparently she'd admitted to knowing what Dustin was doing to Autumn and did nothing about it.

Sky turned to the back of the newspaper and began to search the classified ads. Accepting the fact of what her mother did wasn't easy but she had to move passed the tragedy.

There was no time to stress over what had happened. Sky had a new dilemma: Providing for two siblings that only had her to count on.

Social services agreed to let Sky put her siblings in her custody and told her that welfare would assist her by giving her three hundred dollars a month in cash, along with four hundred dollars in food stamps.

Sky knew that there was no way for the three of them to survive off of that little money and still be able to pay the bills.

She looked down at the paper and circled a few potential jobs and found joy in the fact that at least she would let no more harm come her sibling's way.

There was a knock at the door.

Ever since the case made the news, reporters from all over had been trying to interview her and Autumn.

Sky didn't feel like dealing with the madness so she ignored the knocking.

"Knock... Knock... Knock... Knock."

Whoever it was at the door was persistent.

"Knock... Knock... Knock... Knock."

Sky looked at the door.

"Oh Lord, I don't feel like dealing with these people."

Roughly she closed the newspaper and got up and walked over to the door and yelled through the door.

"Can you please leave us alone right now? We don't feel like talking."

"Sky?" screamed out the person on the other side of the door.

Sky froze. The voice sounded very familiar but Sky stood quiet.

The person spoke again.

"Sky please open the door. I really need to talk to you."

The voice sounded like it belonged to Danielle. Sky got on her tippy toes and looked through the peephole and saw Danielle. Sky felt something tighten up in her chest and she stood behind the door unsure of what to do. Now wasn't the time for Danielle's mess.

Danielle spoke again.

"Sky please just open the door, I promise you that I am over what happened with Calvin."

Sky closed her eyes. She wasn't sure if she could believe her because there was no other reason why she could be there. A bit of a fire sparked in the pit of Sky's stomach. She had done no intentionally harm to Danielle and she felt like there was no reason to be hiding from the girl.

Sky grabbed the door handle and pulled the door open. Danielle stood there with a sympathetic face.

"Sky please forgive me... I was wrong for what I did... it wasn't your fault. Calvin was to blame and that's why I filed for a divorce."

Sky stood there with a tight face looking at her.

Danielle swallowed what looked like a lump of pride.

"I know you're really mad at me, but right now is not the time for that."

She raised her arm and handed Sky a document.

"I read in the newspaper everything that happened and I just came to tell you that I talked to my supervisor, and you can start at the Post Office as soon as you fill out this application."

Sky looked down at the application. The job would help her out so much but she didn't know if she could forgive Danielle.

Slowly Sky reached out and took the application into her hand.

"I'll think about it Danielle, and thank you for the gesture."

Sky started to close the door.

"Hold on... Hold on... Hold on Sky. One more thing."

Danielle reached into her pocket and pulled out Sky's butterfly pendant necklace along with a small envelope.

Sky's heart thumped and then Danielle recited the words that Sky's father recited back when they fought at Sky's sweet sixteen party.

"Sky, I know you are upset right now and you really don't want to hear much, but can you find the strength to forgive this young lady in front of you? Remember Amber Sky,

everybody deserves forgiveness because everybody makes mistakes..."

Tears came to Sky's eyes. Danielle held the necklace out. Sky took it. And then she handed Sky the envelope. Sky opened it and saw a check made out to her for over nine thousand dollars. While she was looking at it, Danielle spoke.

"I took up a collection down at the post office and this is what I came up with."

Sky looked up at her.

"Remember Sky, you can't let them get you down cause you got Girl Power."

Sky melted and tears of joy fell down her face.

"I forgive you Danielle..."

They gave each other a hug.

"Girl Power." Cried Sky.

And from that day forward, they never let anything else come in between them.

AMBER SKY
A.R. DASH

AMBER SKY
A.R. DASH

AMBER SKY
A.R. DASH

OTHER TITLES BY A.R. DASH

MY MOTHER'S DIARY

AND THE BOOK THAT'S THE PERFECT GIFT
FOR ANYONE

THE CRYSTAL DIAMOND DIARY

www.ingramcontent.com/pod-product-compliance
Lightning Source LLC
Chambersburg PA
CBHW060621070426
42447CB00040B/1392